DOVER · THRIFT · EDITIONS

The Heart of Happy Hollow

Paul Laurence Dunbar

DOVER PUBLICATIONS, INC.
Mineola, New York

DOVER THRIFT EDITIONS

GENERAL EDITOR: MARY CAROLYN WALDREP
EDITOR OF THIS VOLUME: JANET BAINE KOPITO

Bibliographical Note

This Dover edition, first published in 2014, is an unabridged republication of the work originally published by Dodd, Mead and Company, New York, in 1904. The illustrations from the original edition have been omitted from the Dover edition. A Note has been provided specially for this edition.

International Standard Book Number

ISBN-13: 978-0-486-49635-1
ISBN-10: 0-486-49635-X

Manufactured in the United States by Courier Corporation
49635X01   2014
www.doverpublications.com

To My Friend

EZRA M. KUHNS

Note

Paul Laurence Dunbar (1872–1906) was born in Dayton, Ohio, the son of former slaves who divorced when he was a child. In high school, Dunbar was elected class president, and he founded and edited the school newspaper. His early successes publishing his poetry led to a literary career during which he produced essays, plays, and short stories, as well as lyrics for *In Dahomey* (1903), the first play written by African Americans and performed on Broadway. With patrons and supporters that included Orville and Wilbur Wright (high school acquaintances of Dunbar's) and the literary critic William Dean Howells, and works published in *The Saturday Evening Post* and *Harper's Weekly,* Dunbar rapidly gained a following. After presenting his writings on a tour of England, Dunbar returned to the United States, where he met and married a teacher and fellow poet, Alice Ruth Moore. After moving to Washington, D.C., to work at the Library of Congress, Dunbar was diagnosed with tuberculosis. Another move, to Denver, did not improve his declining health as hoped for, and Dunbar returned to Dayton, his birthplace, where he died at the age of thirty-three.

Late nineteenth century American literature was experiencing an interest in the regional cultures of the U.S., and Dunbar responded to this trend by incorporating Southern dialect in both his poetry and prose. However, Dunbar also produced serious literary works that had a decidedly more refined tone, and some critics and readers looked askance at his use of southern African American dialects (although to some readers, this lent a more "authentic" tone). This tension between the two literary styles has had a lasting impact on Dunbar's literary legacy.

The Heart of Happy Hollow, which appeared in 1904, includes sixteen of the author's stories. In his Foreword to the collection, Paul Laurence Dunbar declares that Happy Hollow exists "wherever Negroes colonise . . . wherever laughter and tears rub elbows day by day." It is home to "the hod carrier, the porter, and the waiter," and "the picnic and the excursion are the chief summer diversion." Evoking a way of life experienced by African Americans in the decades after the Civil War, Dunbar's stories contain echoes of that not-so-distant past—the horrors of slavery and the damage done by racial hatred, as well as the challenges of a "free people" finding their place in a society that will not easily accept them. And, in spite of their shared past, some of the African American characters in *The Heart of Happy Hollow* encounter economic and societal divisions *between* blacks that further complicate their lives.

In "The Scapegoat," Dunbar examines small-town politics and corruption that lead to class wars among African Americans. When a stranger arrives in the "sleepy little town of Miltonville," awakening the place from its "long post-bellum slumber" in "The Mission of Mr. Scatters," the naïve populace is taught a painful lesson. "Old Abe's Conversion" pits a father against his son in a struggle to understand the true meaning of their religious beliefs. In an unexpectedly ironic twist, the brief monologue, in dialect, in "The Race Question" turns out to concern horse racing; in spite of his protestations about racing being "De work of de devil," the speaker offers a running commentary on the jockey's actions. "The Wisdom of Silence" reveals the difficulties faced by a former slave as he tries to build a successful life without the assistance offered by his former master: "He would not go to his master. Anything rather than that." Racial prejudice leads to tragic consequences in "The Lynching of Jube Benson," a gripping tale in which the narrator admits, "I could only think of him as a monster. It's tradition." In these and the other stories in *The Heart of Happy Hollow,* Paul Laurence Dunbar leaves an indelible imprint on African American literature by creating realistic and unsentimental stories that reveal a deep understanding of the legacy of oppression.

Foreword

HAPPY HOLLOW; are you wondering where it is? Wherever Negroes colonise in the cities or villages, north or south, wherever the hod carrier, the porter, and the waiter are the society men of the town; wherever the picnic and the excursion are the chief summer diversion, and the revival the winter time of repentance, wherever the cheese cloth veil obtains at a wedding, and the little white hearse goes by with black mourners in the one carriage behind, there—there—is Happy Hollow. Wherever laughter and tears rub elbows day by day, and the spirit of labour and laziness shake hands, there—there—is Happy Hollow, and of some of it may the following pages show the heart.

THE AUTHOR

Contents

The Heart of
Happy Hollow

I

THE SCAPEGOAT

I

THE LAW IS USUALLY SUPPOSED to be a stern mistress, not to be lightly wooed, and yielding only to the most ardent pursuit. But even law, like love, sits more easily on some natures than on others.

This was the case with Mr. Robinson Asbury. Mr. Asbury had started life as a bootblack in the growing town of Cadgers. From this he had risen one step and become porter and messenger in a barber-shop. This rise fired his ambition, and he was not content until he had learned to use the shears and the razor and had a chair of his own. From this, in a man of Robinson's temperament, it was only a step to a shop of his own, and he placed it where it would do the most good.

Fully one-half of the population of Cadgers was composed of Negroes, and with their usual tendency to colonise, a tendency encouraged, and in fact compelled, by circumstances, they had gathered into one part of the town. Here in alleys, and streets as dirty and hardly wider, they thronged like ants.

It was in this place that Mr. Asbury set up his shop, and he won the hearts of his prospective customers by putting up the significant sign, "Equal Rights Barber-Shop." This legend was quite unnecessary, because there was only one race about, to patronise the place. But it was a delicate sop to the people's vanity, and it served its purpose.

Asbury came to be known as a clever fellow, and his business grew. The shop really became a sort of club, and, on Saturday nights especially, was the gathering-place of the men of the whole Negro quarter. He kept the illustrated and race journals there, and

1

those who cared neither to talk nor listen to someone else might see pictured the doings of high society in very short skirts or read in the Negro papers how Miss Boston had entertained Miss Blueford to tea on such and such an afternoon. Also, he kept the policy returns, which was wise, if not moral.

It was his wisdom rather more than his morality that made the party managers after a while cast their glances toward him as a man who might be useful to their interests. It would be well to have a man—a shrewd, powerful man—down in that part of the town who could carry his people's vote in his vest pocket, and who at any time its delivery might be needed, could hand it over without hesitation. Asbury seemed that man, and they settled upon him. They gave him money, and they gave him power and patronage. He took it all silently and he carried out his bargain faithfully. His hands and his lips alike closed tightly when there was anything within them. It was not long before he found himself the big Negro of the district and, of necessity, of the town. The time came when, at a critical moment, the managers saw that they had not reckoned without their host in choosing this barber of the black district as the leader of his people.

Now, so much success must have satisfied any other man. But in many ways Mr. Asbury was unique. For a long time he himself had done very little shaving—except of notes, to keep his hand in. His time had been otherwise employed. In the evening hours he had been wooing the coquettish Dame Law, and, wonderful to say, she had yielded easily to his advances.

It was against the advice of his friends that he asked for admission to the bar. They felt that he could do more good in the place where he was.

"You see, Robinson," said old Judge Davis, "it's just like this: If you're not admitted, it'll hurt you with the people; if you are admitted, you'll move uptown to an office and get out of touch with them."

Asbury smiled an inscrutable smile. Then he whispered something into the judge's ear that made the old man wrinkle from his neck up with appreciative smiles.

"Asbury," he said, "you are—you are—well, you ought to be white, that's all. When we find a black man like you we send him to State's prison. If you were white, you'd go to the Senate."

The Negro laughed confidently.

He was admitted to the bar soon after, whether by merit or by connivance is not to be told.

"Now he will move uptown," said the black community. "Well, that's the way with a coloured man when he gets a start."

But they did not know Asbury Robinson yet. He was a man of surprises, and they were destined to disappointment. He did not move uptown. He built an office in a small open space next his shop, and there hung out his shingle.

"I will never desert the people who have done so much to elevate me," said Mr. Asbury. "I will live among them and I will die among them."

This was a strong card for the barber-lawyer. The people seized upon the statement as expressing a nobility of an altogether unique brand.

They held a mass meeting and indorsed him. They made resolutions that extolled him, and the Negro band came around and serenaded him, playing various things in varied time.

All this was very sweet to Mr. Asbury, and the party managers chuckled with satisfaction and said, "That Asbury, that Asbury!"

Now there is a fable extant of a man who tried to please everybody, and his failure is a matter of record. Robinson Asbury was not more successful. But be it said that his ill success was due to no fault or shortcoming of his.

For a long time his growing power had been looked upon with disfavour by the coloured law firm of Bingo & Latchett. Both Mr. Bingo and Mr. Latchett themselves aspired to be Negro leaders in Cadgers, and they were delivering Emancipation Day orations and riding at the head of processions when Mr. Asbury was blacking boots. Is it any wonder, then, that they viewed with alarm his sudden rise? They kept their counsel, however, and treated with him, for it was best. They allowed him his scope without open revolt until the day upon which he hung out his shingle. This was the last straw. They could stand no more. Asbury had stolen their other chances from them, and now he was poaching upon the last of their preserves. So Mr. Bingo and Mr. Latchett put their heads together to plan the downfall of their common enemy.

The plot was deep and embraced the formation of an opposing faction made up of the best Negroes of the town. It would have looked too much like what it was for the gentlemen to show themselves in the matter, and so they took into their confidence Mr. Isaac Morton, the principal of the coloured school, and it was under his ostensible leadership that the new faction finally came into being.

Mr. Morton was really an innocent young man, and he had ideals which should never have been exposed to the air. When the wily confederates came to him with their plan he believed that his worth had been recognised, and at last he was to be what Nature destined him for—a leader.

The better class of Negroes—by that is meant those who were particularly envious of Asbury's success—flocked to the new man's standard. But whether the race be white or black, political virtue is always in a minority, so Asbury could afford to smile at the force arrayed against him.

The new faction met together and resolved. They resolved, among other things, that Mr. Asbury was an enemy to his race and a menace to civilisation. They decided that he should be abolished; but, as they couldn't get out an injunction against him, and as he had the whole undignified but still voting black belt behind him, he went serenely on his way.

"They're after you hot and heavy, Asbury," said one of his friends to him.

"Oh, yes," was the reply, "they're after me, but after a while I'll get so far away that they'll be running in front."

"It's all the best people, they say."

"Yes. Well, it's good to be one of the best people, but your vote only counts one just the same."

The time came, however, when Mr. Asbury's theory was put to the test. The Cadgerites celebrated the first of January as Emancipation Day. On this day there was a large procession, with speechmaking in the afternoon and fireworks at night. It was the custom to concede the leadership of the coloured people of the town to the man who managed to lead the procession. For two years past this honour had fallen, of course, to Robinson Asbury, and there had been no disposition on the part of anybody to try conclusions with him.

Mr. Morton's faction changed all this. When Asbury went to work to solicit contributions for the celebration, he suddenly became aware that he had a fight upon his hands. All the better-class Negroes were staying out of it. The next thing he knew was that plans were on foot for a rival demonstration.

"Oh," he said to himself, "that's it, is it? Well, if they want a fight they can have it."

He had a talk with the party managers, and he had another with Judge Davis.

"All I want is a little lift, judge," he said, "and I'll make 'em think the sky has turned loose and is vomiting niggers."

The judge believed that he could do it. So did the party managers. Asbury got his lift. Emancipation Day came.

There were two parades. At least, there was one parade and the shadow of another. Asbury's, however, was not the shadow. There was a great deal of substance about it—substance made up of many people, many banners, and numerous bands. He did not have the best people. Indeed, among his cohorts there were a good many of the pronounced rag-tag and bobtail. But he had noise and numbers. In such cases, nothing more is needed. The success of Asbury's side of the affair did everything to confirm his friends in their good opinion of him.

When he found himself defeated, Mr. Silas Bingo saw that it would be policy to placate his rival's just anger against him. He called upon him at his office the day after the celebration.

"Well, Asbury," he said, "you beat us, didn't you?"

"It wasn't a question of beating," said the other calmly. "It was only an inquiry as to who were the people—the few or the many."

"Well, it was well done, and you've shown that you are a manager. I confess that I haven't always thought that you were doing the wisest thing in living down here and catering to this class of people when you might, with your ability, to be much more to the better class."

"What do they base their claims of being better on?"

"Oh, there ain't any use discussing that. We can't get along without you, we see that. So I, for one, have decided to work with you for harmony."

"Harmony. Yes, that's what we want."

"If I can do anything to help you at any time, why you have only to command me."

"I am glad to find such a friend in you. Be sure, if I ever need you, Bingo, I'll call on you."

"And I'll be ready to serve you."

Asbury smiled when his visitor was gone. He smiled, and knitted his brow. "I wonder what Bingo's got up his sleeve," he said. "He'll bear watching."

It may have been pride at his triumph, it may have been gratitude at his helpers, but Asbury went into the ensuing campaign with reckless enthusiasm. He did the most daring things for the party's sake. Bingo, true to his promise, was ever at his side ready to serve him. Finally, association and immunity made danger less fearsome; the rival no longer appeared a menace.

With the generosity born of obstacles overcome, Asbury determined to forgive Bingo and give him a chance. He let him in on a deal, and from that time they worked amicably together until the election came and passed.

It was a close election and many things had had to be done, but there were men there ready and waiting to do them. They were successful, and then the first cry of the defeated party was, as usual, "Fraud! Fraud!" The cry was taken up by the jealous, the disgruntled, and the virtuous.

Someone remembered how two years ago the registration books had been stolen. It was known upon good authority that money had been freely used. Men held up their hands in horror at the suggestion that the Negro vote had been juggled with, as if that were a new thing. From their pulpits ministers denounced the machine and bade their hearers rise and throw off the yoke of a corrupt municipal government. One of those sudden fevers of reform had taken possession of the town and threatened to destroy the successful party.

They began to look around them. They must purify themselves. They must give the people some tangible evidence of their own yearnings after purity. They looked around them for a sacrifice to lay upon the altar of municipal reform. Their eyes fell upon Mr. Bingo. No, he was not big enough. His blood was too scant to wash away the political stains. Then they looked into each other's eyes and turned their gaze away to let it fall upon Mr. Asbury. They really hated to do it. But there must be a scapegoat. The god from the Machine commanded them to slay him.

Robinson Asbury was charged with many crimes—with all that he had committed and some that he had not. When Mr. Bingo saw what was afoot he threw himself heart and soul into the work of his old rival's enemies. He was of incalculable use to them.

Judge Davis refused to have anything to do with the matter. But in spite of his disapproval it went on. Asbury was indicted and tried. The evidence was all against him, and no one gave more damaging testimony than his friend, Mr. Bingo. The judge's charge was favourable to the defendant, but the current of popular opinion could not be entirely stemmed. The jury brought in a verdict of guilty.

"Before I am sentenced, judge, I have a statement to make to the court. It will take less than ten minutes."

"Go on, Robinson," said the judge kindly.

Asbury started, in a monotonous tone, a recital that brought the prosecuting attorney to his feet in a minute. The judge waved him down, and sat transfixed by a sort of fascinated horror as the convicted man went on. The before-mentioned attorney drew a knife and started for the prisoner's dock. With difficulty he was restrained. A dozen faces in the court-room were red and pale by turns.

"He ought to be killed," whispered Mr. Bingo audibly.

Robinson Asbury looked at him and smiled, and then he told a few things of him. He gave the ins and outs of some of the misdemeanours of which he stood accused. He showed who were the men behind the throne. And still, pale and transfixed, Judge Davis waited for his own sentence.

Never were ten minutes so well taken up. It was a tale of rottenness and corruption in high places told simply and with the stamp of truth upon it.

He did not mention the judge's name. But he had torn the mask from the face of every other man who had been concerned in his downfall. They had shorn him of his strength, but they had forgotten that he was yet able to bring the roof and pillars tumbling about their heads.

The judge's voice shook as he pronounced sentence upon his old ally—a year in State's prison.

Some people said it was too light, but the judge knew what it was to wait for the sentence of doom, and he was grateful and sympathetic.

When the sheriff led Asbury away the judge hastened to have a short talk with him.

"I'm sorry, Robinson," he said, "and I want to tell you that you were no more guilty than the rest of us. But why did you spare me?"

"Because I knew you were my friend," answered the convict.

"I tried to be, but you were the first man that I've ever known since I've been in politics who ever gave me any decent return for friendship."

"I reckon you're about right, judge."

In politics, party reform usually lies in making a scapegoat of someone who is only as criminal as the rest, but a little weaker. Asbury's friends and enemies had succeeded in making him bear the burden of all the party's crimes, but their reform was hardly a success, and their protestations of a change of heart were received with doubt. Already there were those who began to pity the victim and to say that he had been hardly dealt with.

Mr. Bingo was not of these; but he found, strange to say, that his opposition to the idea went but a little way, and that even with Asbury out of his path he was a smaller man than he was before. Fate was strong against him. His poor, prosperous humanity could not enter the lists against a martyr. Robinson Asbury was now a martyr.

II

A year is not a long time. It was short enough to prevent people from forgetting Robinson, and yet long enough for their pity to grow strong as they remembered. Indeed, he was not gone a year. Good behaviour cut two months off the time of his sentence, and by the time people had come around to the notion that he was really the greatest and smartest man in Cadgers he was at home again.

He came back with no flourish of trumpets, but quietly, humbly. He went back again into the heart of the black district. His business had deteriorated during his absence, but he put new blood and new life into it. He did not go to work in the shop himself, but, taking down the shingle that had swung idly before his office door during his imprisonment, he opened the little room as a news- and cigar-stand.

Here anxious, pitying custom came to him and he prospered again. He was very quiet. Uptown hardly knew that he was again in Cadgers, and it knew nothing whatever of his doings.

"I wonder why Asbury is so quiet," they said to one another. "It isn't like him to be quiet." And they felt vaguely uneasy about him.

So many people had begun to say, "Well, he was a mighty good fellow after all."

Mr. Bingo expressed the opinion that Asbury was quiet because he was crushed, but others expressed doubt as to this. There are calms and calms, some after and some before the storm. Which was this?

They waited a while, and, as no storm came, concluded that this must be the after-quiet. Bingo, reassured, volunteered to go and seek confirmation of this conclusion.

He went, and Asbury received him with an indifferent, not to say, impolite, demeanour.

"Well, we're glad to see you back, Asbury," said Bingo patronisingly. He had variously demonstrated his inability to lead during his rival's absence and was proud of it. "What are you going to do?"

"I'm going to work."

"That's right. I reckon you'll stay out of politics."

"What could I do even if I went in?"

"Nothing now, of course; but I didn't know—"

He did not see the gleam in Asbury's half shut eyes. He only marked his humility, and he went back swelling with the news.

"Completely crushed—all the run taken out of him," was his report.

The black district believed this, too, and a sullen, smouldering anger took possession of them. Here was a good man ruined. Some of the people whom he had helped in his former days—some of the rude, coarse people of the low quarter who were still sufficiently unenlightened to be grateful—talked among themselves and offered to get up a demonstration for him. But he denied them. No, he wanted nothing of the kind. It would only bring him into unfavourable notice. All he wanted was that they would always be his friends and would stick by him.

They would to the death.

There were again two factions in Cadgers. The schoolmaster could not forget how once on a time he had been made a tool of by Mr. Bingo. So he revolted against his rule and set himself up as the leader of an opposing clique. The fight had been long and strong, but had ended with odds slightly in Bingo's favour.

But Mr. Morton did not despair. As the first of January and Emancipation Day approached, he arrayed his hosts, and the fight for supremacy became fiercer than ever. The schoolteacher brought the school-children in for chorus singing, secured an able orator, and the best essayist in town. With all this, he was formidable.

Mr. Bingo knew that he had the fight of his life on his hands, and he entered with fear as well as zest. He, too, found an orator, but he was not sure that he was as good as Morton's. There was no doubt but that his essayist was not. He secured a band, but still he felt unsatisfied. He had hardly done enough, and for the schoolmaster to beat him now meant his political destruction.

It was in this state of mind that he was surprised to receive a visit from Mr. Asbury.

"I reckon you're surprised to see me here," said Asbury, smiling.

"I am pleased, I know." Bingo was astute.

"Well, I just dropped in on business."

"To be sure, to be sure, Asbury. What can I do for you?"

"It's more what I can do for you that I came to talk about," was the reply.

"I don't believe I understand you."

"Well, it's plain enough. They say that the school-teacher is giving you a pretty hard fight."

"Oh, not so hard."

"No man can be too sure of winning, though. Mr. Morton once did me a mean turn when he started the faction against me."

Bingo's heart gave a great leap, and then stopped for the fraction of a second.

"You were in it, of course," pursued Asbury, "but I can look over your part in it in order to get even with the man who started it."

It was true, then, thought Bingo gladly. He did not know. He wanted revenge for his wrongs and upon the wrong man. How well the schemer had covered his tracks! Asbury should have his revenge and Morton would be the sufferer.

"Of course, Asbury, you know what I did I did innocently."

"Oh, yes, in politics we are all lambs and the wolves are only to be found in the other party. We'll pass that, though. What I want to say is that I can help you to make your celebration an overwhelming success. I still have some influence down in my district."

"Certainly, and very justly, too. Why, I should be delighted with your aid. I could give you a prominent place in the procession."

"I don't want it; I don't want to appear in this at all. All I want is revenge. You can have all the credit, but let me down my enemy."

Bingo was perfectly willing, and, with their heads close together, they had a long and close consultation. When Asbury was gone, Mr. Bingo lay back in his chair and laughed. "I'm a slick duck," he said.

From that hour Mr. Bingo's cause began to take on the appearance of something very like a boom. More bands were hired. The interior of the State was called upon and a more eloquent orator secured. The crowd hastened to array itself on the growing side.

With surprised eyes, the schoolmaster beheld the wonder of it, but he kept to his own purpose with dogged insistence, even when he saw that he could not turn aside the overwhelming defeat that threatened him. But in spite of his obstinacy, his hours were dark and bitter. Asbury worked like a mole, all underground, but he was indefatigable. Two days before the celebration time everything was perfected for the biggest demonstration that Cadgers had ever known. All the next day and night he was busy among his allies.

On the morning of the great day, Mr. Bingo, wonderfully caparisoned, rode down to the hall where the parade was to form. He was early. No one had yet come. In an hour a score of men all told had collected. Another hour passed, and no more had come. Then there smote upon his ear the sound of music. They were coming at last. Bringing his sword to his shoulder, he rode forward to the middle of the street. Ah, there they were. But—but—could he believe his eyes? They were going in another direction, and at their head rode—Morton! He gnashed his teeth in fury. He had been led into a trap and betrayed. The procession passing had been his—all his. He heard them cheering, and then, oh! climax of infidelity, he saw his own orator go past in a carriage, bowing and smiling to the crowd.

There was no doubting who had done this thing. The hand of Asbury was apparent in it. He must have known the truth all along, thought Bingo. His allies left him one by one for the other hall, and he rode home in a humiliation deeper than he had ever known before.

Asbury did not appear at the celebration. He was at his little news-stand all day.

In a day or two the defeated aspirant had further cause to curse his false friend. He found that not only had the people defected from him, but that the thing had been so adroitly managed that he appeared to be in fault, and three-fourths of those who knew him were angry at some supposed grievance. His cup of bitterness was full when his partner, a quietly ambitious man, suggested that they dissolve their relations.

His ruin was complete.

The lawyer was not alone in seeing Asbury's hand in his downfall. The party managers saw it too, and they met together to discuss the dangerous factor which, while it appeared to slumber, was so terribly awake. They decided that he must be appeased, and they visited him.

He was still busy at his news-stand. They talked to him adroitly, while he sorted papers and kept an impassive face. When they were all done, he looked up for a moment and replied, "You know, gentlemen, as an ex-convict I am not in politics."

Some of them had the grace to flush.

"But you can use your influence," they said.

"I am not in politics," was his only reply.

And the spring elections were coming on. Well, they worked hard, and he showed no sign. He treated with neither one party nor the other. "Perhaps," thought the managers, "he is out of politics," and they grew more confident.

It was nearing eleven o'clock on the morning of election when a cloud no bigger than a man's hand appeared upon the horizon. It came from the direction of the black district. It grew, and the managers of the party in power looked at it, fascinated by an ominous dread. Finally it began to rain Negro voters, and as one man they voted against their former candidates. Their organisation was perfect. They simply came, voted, and left, but they overwhelmed everything. Not one of the party that had damned Robinson Asbury was left in power save old Judge Davis. His majority was overwhelming.

The generalship that had engineered the thing was perfect. There were loud threats against the newsdealer. But no one bothered him except a reporter. The reporter called to see just how it was done. He found Asbury very busy sorting papers. To the newspaper man's questions he had only this reply, "I am not in politics, sir."

But Cadgers had learned its lesson.

II

ONE CHRISTMAS AT SHILOH

MARTHA MARIA MIXON was a "widder lady." So she described
herself whenever anyone asked her as to her status in life. To her
more intimate friends she confided that she was not a "weed widder," but one of the "grass" variety. The story of how her husband,
Madison, had never been "No 'count, even befo' de wah," and of
his rapid degeneration thereafter, was vividly told.

"De fact of de mattah is," Mrs. Mixon was wont to say, "my
man, Madison, was nevah no han' to wo'k. He was de settin'-
downest man you evah seed. Hit wouldn't 'a' been so bad, but
Madison was a lakly man, an' his tongue wah smoothah dan ile; so
hit t'wan't no shakes fu' him to fool ol' Mas' 'bout his wo'k an' git
erlong des erbout ez he pleased. Mas' Madison Mixon, hisse'f, was
a mighty 'dulgent so't o' man, an' he liked a laugh bettah dan anyone in de worl'. Well, my man could mek him laugh, an' dat was
enough fu' him. I used to lectuah dat man much 'bout his onshifless
ways, but he des went erlong, twell bimeby hyeah come de wah
an' evahthing was broke up. Den w'en hit come time dat Madison
had to scramble fu' hisself, dey wa'nt no scramble in him. He des'
wouldn't wo'k an' I had to do evahthing. He allus had what he
called some gret scheme, but deh nevah seemed to come to nuffin,
an' once when he got de folks to put some money in somep'n' dat
broke up, dey come put' nigh tahin' an' featherin' him. Finally, I
des got morchully tiahed o' dat man's ca'in' on, an' I say to him
one day, 'Madison,' I say, 'I'm tiahed of all dis foo'ishness, an' I'm
gwine up Norf whaih I kin live an' be somebody. Ef evah you mek
a man out o' yo'se'f, an' want me, de Bible say 'Seek an' you shell
receive.' Cause even den I was a mighty han' to c'ote de Scripters.
Well, I lef' him, an' Norf I come, 'dough it jes' nigh broke my

13

hea't, fu' I sho did love dat black man. De las' thing I hyeahed o' him, he had des learned to read an' write an' wah runnin' fu' de Legislater 'twell de Klu Klux got aftah him; den I think he 'signed de nomernation."

This was Martha's story, and the reason that there was no Mr. Mixon with her when she came North, drifted from place to place and finally became one of New York's large black contingent from the South. To her the lessons of slavery had not been idle ones. Industrious, careful, and hard-working, she soon became prosperous, and when, hunting a spiritual home she settled upon Shiloh Chapel, she was welcomed there as a distinct addition to the large and active membership.

Shiloh was not one of the fashionable churches of the city, but it was primarily a church home for any Southern negro, for in it were representatives of every one of the old slaveholding States. Its pastor was one of those who had not yet got beyond the belief that any temporal preparation for the preaching of the Gospel was unnecessary. It was still his firm trust, and often his boast, that if one opened his mouth the Lord would fill it, and it grew to be a settled idea that the Lord filled his acceptably, for his converts were many and his congregation increased.

The Rev. Silas Todbury's education may have been deficient in other matters, but one thing he knew, and knew thoroughly—the disposition of his people. He knew just what weaknesses, longings, and desires their recent bondage had left with them, and with admirable shrewdness contrived to meet them. He knew that in preaching they wanted noise, emotion, and fire; that in the preacher they wanted free-heartedness and cordiality. He knew that when Christmas came they wanted a great rally, somewhat approaching, at least, the rousing times both spiritual and temporal that they had had back on the old plantation, when Christmas meant a week of pleasurable excitement. Knowing the last so well, it was with commendable foresight that he began early his preparations for a big time on a certain Christmas not long ago.

"I tell you people," he said to his congregation, "we's goin' to have a reg'lar 'Benjamin's mess'!"

The coloured folk, being not quite sure of the quotation, laughed heartily, exclaiming in admiration of their pastor, "Dat Todbu'y is sholy one mess hisse'f."

"Now any of de sistahs dat's willin' to he'p mek dis comin'

Chris'mus a real sho 'nough one, 'll 'blige me by meetin' me in de basement of de chu'ch aftah services. De brothahs kin go 'long home 'twell dey called fu'."

There was another outburst of merriment at this sally, and it was a good-natured score or more of sisters who a little later met the pastor as agreed. Among them was Martha Maria Mixon, for she was very close to her pastor, and for many a day had joyed his clerical heart with special dinners.

"Ah," said the preacher, rubbing his hands, "Sistah Marthy, I see you's on han' ez usual to he'p me out, an' you, too, Sis Jinny, an' Sis Dicey," he added, quick to note the signs of any incipient jealousy, and equally ready to check it. "We's all hyeah, de faithful few, an' we's all ready fu' wo'k."

The sisters beamed and nodded.

"Well, we goin' to have some'p'n evah night, beginnin' wid Chris'mus night, straight on endurin' of de week, an' I want to separate you all into companies fu' to take chawge of each night. Now, I's a-goin' to have a powahful preachah f'om de Souf wid us, an' I want you all to show him what we kin do. On Chris'mus day we goin' to have a sermont at de chu'ch an' a festabal in de evenin' wid a Chris'mus tree. Sis' Marthy, I want you to boa'd de minister."

"La, Brothah Todbu'y, I don't scarcely feel lak I's 'portant 'nough fu' dat," said Mrs. Mixon modestly, "but I'll do de bes' I kin. I hatter be lak de widder's mice in de scuse o' meal."

"We ain't got no doubt 'bout what you able to do, Sis Marthy," and the pastor passed to the appointment of his other committees. After evening services the brothers were similarly called in consultation and appointed to their respective duties.

To the black people to whom these responsibilities were thus turned over, joy came, and with it the vision of other days—the vision of the dear old days, the hard old days back there in the South, when they had looked forward to their Christmas from year to year. Then it had been a time of sadness as well as of joy, for they knew that though the week was full of pleasure, after it was over must come separation and sadness. For this was the time when those who were to be hired out, loaned, or given away, were to change their homes. So even while they danced they sighed, and while they shouted they moaned. Now there was no such repressing fact to daunt them. Christmas would come. They would enjoy themselves, and after it was over would go back to the same homes to live through the round of months in the midst of familiar faces and among their own old loved ones. The thought gave sweetness to their labour, and the responsibilities devolving upon them imbued the sacred holiday with a meaning and charm that it had never had before for them. They bubbled over with importance and with the glory of it. A sister and a brother could not meet without a friendly banter.

"Hi, Sis' Dicey," Brother Williams would call out across the fence to his neighbour, "I don' believe you doin' anything to'ds dat Chris'mus celebration. Evah time I sees you, you's in de washtub tryin' to mek braid an' meat fo' dat no 'count man o' yo'n."

Sister Dicey's laugh rang out loud and musical before she replied, "Nevah you min', Brothah Williams. I don' see yo' back bowed so much by de yoke."

"Oh, honey, I's labo'in' even ef you do'n know it, but you'll see it on de day."

"I 'low you labo'in' de mos' to git dat wife o' yo'n a new dress," and her tormentor's guffaw seemed to admit some such benevolent intention.

In the corners of every house where the younger and more worldly-minded people congregated there was much whispering and giggling, for they had their own plans for Christmas outside of the church affair.

"You goin' to give me de pleasure of yo' comp'ny to de dance aftah de festabal?" some ardent and early swain would murmur to his lady love, and the whisper would fly back in well-feigned affright, "Heish, man, you want to have Brothah Todbu'y chu'chin' me?" But if the swain persisted, there was little chance of his being ultimately refused. So the world, the flesh, and the devil kept pace with the things of the spirit in the great preparation.

Meanwhile Martha Maria Mixon went her own way, working hard, fixing and observing. She had determined to excel herself this time, and not only should her part at the church be above reproach, but the entertainment which she would give that strange preacher would be a thing long to be remembered. And so, almost startled at all that Shiloh was preparing for his reception, hoary Christmas approached.

All New York was a dazzling bazar through which the people thronged ceaselessly, tumultuously. Everyone was a child again;

holly wreaths with the red berries gleaming amid the green were everywhere, and the white streets were gay with laughter and bustle and life.

On the night before the great day Martha sat before her fire and hummed softly to herself. There was a smile upon her face, for she had worked and worked well, and now all was ready and to her entire satisfaction. Something which shall be nameless simmered in a tin cup on the back of the stove before her, and every now and then she broke her reverie to sip of it. It smelled sweet and pungent and suspicious, but, then—this was Christmas Eve. She was half drowsing when a brisk knock startled her into wakefulness. Thinking it was one of the neighbours in for a call she bade the visitor enter, without moving. There was a stamping of feet, and the door opened and a black man covered with snow stood before her. He said nothing. Martha rubbed her eyes and stared at him, and then she looked at the cup accusingly, and from it back to the man. Then she rubbed her eyes again.

"Wha—wha——" she stammered, rising slowly.

"Don' you know me, Marthy, don' you know me; an' don' you want to see yo' husban'?"

"Madison Mixon, is dat you in de flesh?"

"It's me, Marthy; you tol' me ef evah I made a man o' myse'f, to seek you. It's been a long road, but I's tried faithful."

All the memories of other days came rushing over Martha in an overwhelming flood. In one moment everything was forgotten save that here stood her long delinquent husband. She threw out her arms and took a step toward him, but he anticipated her further advance and rushing to her clasped her ample form in a close embrace.

"You will tek me back!" he cried, "you will fu'give me!"

"Yes, yes, of co'se, I will, Madison, ef you has made a man of yo'se'f."

"I hopes to prove dat to you."

It was a very pleasant evening that they spent together, and like old times to Martha. Never once did it occur to her that this sudden finding of a husband might be awkward on the morrow when the visitor came to dinner. Nor did she once suspect that Madison might be up to one of his old tricks. She accepted him for just what he said he was and intended to be.

Her first doubt came the next morning when she began to hurry her preparations for church. Madison had been fumbling in his carpet bag and was already respectably dressed. His wife looked at him approvingly, but the glance turned to one of consternation when he stammered forth that he had to go out, as he had some business to attend to.

"What, on de ve'y fust day you hyeah, ain't you goin' to chu'ch wid me?"

"De bus'ness is mighty pressin', but I hopes to see you at chu'ch by de time de services begin. Waih does you set?" His hand was on the door.

Martha sank into a chair and the tears came to her eyes, but she choked them back. She would not let him see how much she was hurt. She told him in a faltering voice where she sat, and he passed out. Then her tears came and flooded away the last hope. She had been so proud to think that she would walk to church with her husband that morning for the first time in so long a while, and now it was all over. For a little while she thought that she would not go, and then the memory of all the preparations she had made and of the new minister came to her, and she went on with her dressing.

The church was crowded that morning when Martha arrived. She looked around in vain for some sight of Madison, but she could see nothing of him, and so she sank into her seat with a sigh. She could just see the new minister drooping in his seat behind the reading desk. He was evidently deep in meditation, for he did not get up during the hymn.

Then Martha heard the Rev. Silas Todbury speaking. His words did not affect her until she found that the whole of his closing sentence was flashing through her brain like a flame. "We will now be exho'ted by de Reverent Madison Mixon."

She couldn't believe her ears, but stared wildly at the pulpit where the new preacher stood. It was Madison. Her first impulse was to rise in her seat and stop him. It was another of his tricks, and he should not profane the church. But his look and voice silenced her and she sank back in amazement.

He preached a powerful sermon, and at its close told something of his life and who he was, and Martha found herself all at once the centre of attention; and her face glowed and her heart burned within her as the people about her nodded and smiled at her through their tears, and hurled "Amen" upon "Amen."

Madison hurried to her side after the services. "I des wanted to s'prise you a little, Marthy," he said.

She was too happy to answer and, pressing his arm very tightly, she walked out among her congratulating friends, and between her husband and the Rev. Silas Todbury went proudly home to her Christmas dinner.

III

THE MISSION OF MR. SCATTERS

It took something just short of a revolution to wake up the sleepy little town of Miltonville. Through the slow, hot days it drowsed along like a lazy dog, only half rousing now and then to snap at some flying rumour, and relapsing at once into its pristine somnolence.

It was not a dreamless sleep, however, that held the town in chains. It had its dreams—dreams of greatness, of wealth, of consequence and of growth. Granted that there was no effort to realise these visions, they were yet there, and, combined with the memory of a past that was not without credit, went far to give tone to its dormant spirit.

It was a real spirit, too; the gallant Bourbon spirit of the old South; of Kentucky when she is most the daughter of Virginia, as was evidenced in the awed respect which all Miltonvillians, white and black alike, showed to Major Richardson in his house on the hill. He was part of the traditions of the place. It was shown in the conservatism of the old white families, and a certain stalwart if reflected self-respect in the older coloured inhabitants.

In all the days since the school had been founded and Mr. Dunkin's marriage to the teacher had raised a brief ripple of excitement, these coloured people had slumbered. They were still slumbering that hot August day, unmindful of the sensation that lay at their very doors, heedless of the portents that said as plain as preaching, "Miltonville, the time is at hand, awake!"

So it was that that afternoon there were only a few loungers, and these not very alert, about the station when the little train wheezed and puffed its way into it. It had been so long since anyone save those whom they knew had alighted at Miltonville that the loungers had lost faith, and with it curiosity, and now they scarcely changed their positions as the little engine stopped with a snort of disgust. But in an instant indifference had fled as the mist before the sun, and every eye on the platform was staring and white. It is the unexpected that always happens, and yet humanity never gets accustomed to it. The loafers, white and black, had assumed a sitting posture, and then they had stood up. For from the cars there had alighted the wonder of a stranger—a Negro stranger, gorgeous of person and attire. He was dressed in a suit of black cloth. A long coat was buttoned close around his tall and robust form. He was dead black, from his shiny top hat to his not less shiny boots, and about him there was the indefinable air of distinction. He stood looking about the platform for a moment, and then stepped briskly and decisively toward the group that was staring at him with wide eyes. There was no hesitation in that step. He walked as a man walks who is not in the habit of being stopped, who has not known what it is to be told, "Thus far shalt thou go and no further."

"Can you tell me where I can find the residence of Mr. Isaac Jackson?" he asked sonorously as he reached the stupefied loungers. His voice was deep and clear.

Someone woke from his astonishment and offered to lead him thither, and together the two started for their destination, the stranger keeping up a running fire of comment on the way. Had his companion been a close observer and known anything about the matter, he would have found the newcomer's English painfully, unforgivably correct. A language should be like an easy shoe on a flexible foot, but to one unused to it, it proves rather a splint on a broken limb. The stranger stalked about in conversational splints until they arrived at Isaac Jackson's door. Then giving his guide a dime, he dismissed him with a courtly bow, and knocked.

It was a good thing that Martha Ann Jackson had the innate politeness of her race well to the fore when she opened the door upon the radiant creature, or she would have given voice to the words that were in her heart: "Good Lawd, what is dis?"

"Is this the residence of Mr. Isaac Jackson?" in the stranger's suavest voice.

"Yes, suh, he live hyeah."

"May I see him? I desire to see him upon some business." He handed her his card, which she carefully turned upside down, glanced at without understanding, and put in her apron pocket as she replied:

"He ain't in jes' now, but ef you'll step in an' wait, I'll sen' one o' de chillen aftah him."

"I thank you, madam, I thank you. I will come in and rest from the fatigue of my journey. I have travelled a long way, and rest in such a pleasant and commodious abode as your own appears to be will prove very grateful to me."

She had been half afraid to invite this resplendent figure into her humble house, but she felt distinctly flattered at his allusion to the home which she had helped Isaac to buy, and by the alacrity with which the stranger accepted her invitation.

She ushered him into the front room, mentally thanking her stars that she had forced the reluctant Isaac to buy a bright new carpet a couple of months before.

A child was despatched to find and bring home the father, while Martha Ann, hastily slipping out of her work-dress and into a starched calico, came in to keep her visitor company.

His name proved to be Scatters, and he was a most entertaining and ingratiating man. It was evident that he had some important business with Isaac Jackson, but that it was mysterious was shown by the guarded way in which he occasionally hinted at it as he tapped the valise he carried and nodded knowingly.

Time had never been when Martha Ann Jackson was so flustered. She was charmed and frightened and flattered. She could only leave Mr. Scatters long enough to give orders to her daughter, Lucy, to prepare such a supper as that household had never seen before; then she returned to sit again at his feet and listen to his words of wisdom.

The supper progressed apace, and the savour of it was already in the stranger's nostrils. Upon this he grew eloquent and was about to divulge his secret to the hungry-eyed woman when the trampling of Isaac's boots upon the walk told him that he had only a little while longer to contain himself, and at the same time to wait for the fragrant supper.

Now, it is seldom that a man is so well impressed with a smooth-tongued stranger as is his wife. Usually his hard-headedness puts him on the defensive against the blandishments of the man who has won his better half's favour, and, however honest the semi-fortunate individual may be, he despises him for his attainments. But it was not so in this case. Isaac had hardly entered the house and received his visitor's warm handclasp before he had become captive to his charm. Business, business—no, his guest had been travelling and he must be both tired and hungry. Isaac would hear of no business until they had eaten. Then, over a pipe, if the gentleman smoked, they might talk at their ease.

Mr. Scatters demurred, but in fact nothing could have pleased him better, and the open smile with which he dropped into his place at the table was very genuine and heartfelt. Genuine, too, were his praises of Lucy's cooking; of her flaky biscuits and mealy potatoes. He was pleased all through and he did not hesitate to say so.

It was a beaming group that finally rose heavily laden from the supper table.

Over a social pipe a little later, Isaac Jackson heard the story that made his eyes bulge with interest and his heart throb with eagerness.

Mr. Scatters began, tapping his host's breast and looking at him fixedly, "You had a brother some years ago named John." It was more like an accusation than a question.

"Yes, suh, I had a brothah John."

"Uh, huh, and that brother migrated to the West Indies."

"Yes, suh, he went out to some o' dem outlandish places."

"Hold on, sir, hold on, I am a West Indian myself."

"I do' mean no erfence, 'ceptin' dat John allus was of a rovin' dispersition."

"Very well, you know no more about your brother after his departure for the West Indies?"

"No, suh."

"Well, it is my mission to tell you the rest of the story. Your brother John landed at Cuba, and after working about some years and living frugally, he went into the coffee business, in which he became rich."

"Rich?"

"Rich, sir."

"Why, bless my soul, who'd 'a evah thought that of John? Why, suh, I'm sho'ly proud to hyeah it. Why don't he come home an' visit a body?"

"Ah, why?" said Mr. Scatters dramatically. "Now comes the most painful part of my mission. 'In the midst of life we are in death.'" Mr. Scatters sighed, Isaac sighed and wiped his eyes. "Two years ago your brother departed this life."

"Was he saved?" Isaac asked in a choked voice. Scatters gave him one startled glance, and then answered hastily, "I am happy to say that he was."

"Poor John! He gone an' me lef'."

"Even in the midst of our sorrows, however, there is always a ray of light. Your brother remembered you in his will."

"Remembered me?"

"Remembered you, and as one of the executors of his estate,"— Mr. Scatters rose and went softly over to his valise, from which he took a large square package. He came back with it, holding it as if it were something sacred,—"as one of the executors of his estate, which is now settled, I was commissioned to bring you this." He tapped the package. "This package, sealed as you see with the seal of Cuba, contains five thousand dollars in notes and bonds."

Isaac gasped and reached for the bundle, but it was withdrawn. "I am, however, not to deliver it to you yet. There are certain formalities which my country demands to be gone through with, after which I deliver my message and return to the fairest of lands, to the Gem of the Antilles. Let me congratulate you, Mr. Jackson, upon your good fortune."

Isaac yielded up his hand mechanically. He was dazed by the vision of this sudden wealth.

"Fi' thousan' dollahs," he repeated.

"Yes, sir, five thousand dollars. It is a goodly sum, and in the meantime, until court convenes, I wish you to recommend some safe place in which to put this money, as I do not feel secure with it about my person, nor would it be secure if it were known to be in your house."

"I reckon Albert Matthews' grocery would be the safes' place fu' it. He's got one o' dem i'on saftes."

"The very place. Let us go there at once, and after that I will not encroach upon your hospitality longer, but attempt to find a hotel."

"Hotel nothin'," said Isaac emphatically. "Ef my house ain't too common, you'll stay right thaih ontwell co't sets."

"This is very kind of you, Mr. Jackson, but really I couldn't think of being such a charge upon you and your good wife."

"'Tain't no charge on us; we'll be glad to have you. Folks hyeah in Miltonville has little enough comp'ny, de Lawd knows."

Isaac spoke the truth, and it was as much the knowledge that he would be the envy of all the town as his gratitude to Scatters that prompted him to prevail upon his visitor to stay.

Scatters was finally persuaded, and the men only paused long enough in the house to tell the curiosity-eaten Martha Ann the news, and then started for Albert Matthews' store. Scatters carried the precious package, and Isaac was armed with an old shotgun lest anyone should suspect their treasure and attack them. Five thousand dollars was not to be carelessly handled!

As soon as the men were gone, Martha Ann started out upon her rounds, and her proud tongue did for the women portion of Miltonville what the visit to Matthews' store did for the men. Did Mrs. So-and-So remember brother John? Indeed she did. And when the story was told, it was a "Well, well, well! he used to be an ol' beau o' mine." Martha Ann found no less than twenty women of her acquaintance for whom her brother John seemed to have entertained tender feelings.

The corner grocery store kept by Albert Matthews was the general gathering-place for the coloured male population of the town. It was a small, one-roomed building, almost filled with barrels, boxes, and casks.

Pride as well as necessity had prompted Isaac to go to the grocery just at this time, when it would be quite the fullest of men. He had not calculated wrongly when he reckoned upon the sensation that would be made by his entrance with the distinguished-looking stranger. The excitement was all the most hungry could have wished for. The men stared at Jackson and his companion with wide-open eyes. They left off chewing tobacco and telling tales. A half-dozen of them forgot to avail themselves of the joy of spitting, and Albert Matthews, the proprietor, a weazened little brown-skinned man, forgot to lay his hand upon the scale in weighing out a pound of sugar.

With a humility that was false on the very face of it, Isaac introduced his guest to the grocer and the three went off together mysteriously into a corner. The matter was duly explained and the object of the visit told. Matthews burned with envy of his neighbour's good fortune.

"I do' reckon, Mistah Scatters, dat we bettah let de othah folks in de sto' know anything 'bout dis hyeah bus'ness of ouahs. I got to be 'sponsible fu dat money, an' I doesn't want to tek no chances."

"You are perfectly right, sir, perfectly right. You are responsible, not only for the money itself, but for the integrity of this seal which means the dignity of government."

Matthews looked sufficiently impressed, and together they all went their way among the barrels and boxes to the corner where the little safe stood. With many turnings and twistings the door was opened, the package inclosed and the safe shut again. Then they all rose solemnly and went behind the counter to sample something that Matthews had. This was necessary as a climax, for they had performed, not a mere deed, but a ceremonial.

"Of course, you'll say nothing about this matter at all, Mr. Matthews," said Scatters, thereby insuring publicity to his affair.

There were a few introductions as the men passed out, but hardly had their backs turned when a perfect storm of comment and inquiry broke about the grocer's head. So it came to pass, that with many mysterious nods and headshakings, Matthews first hinted at and then told the story.

For the first few minutes the men could scarcely believe what they had heard. It was so utterly unprecedented. Then it dawned upon them that it might be so, and discussion and argument ran rife for the next hour.

The story flew like wildfire, there being three things in this world which interest all sorts and conditions of men alike: great wealth, great beauty, and great love. Whenever Mr. Scatters appeared he was greeted with deference and admiration. Any man who had come clear from Cuba on such an errand to their fellow-townsman deserved all honour and respect. His charming manners confirmed, too, all that preconceived notions had said of him. He became a social favourite. It began with Mr. and Mrs. Dunkin's calling upon him. Then followed Alonzo Taft, and when the former two gave a reception for the visitor, his position was assured. Miltonville had not yet arisen to the dignity of having a literary society. He now founded one and opened it himself with an address so beautiful, so eloquent and moving that Mr. Dunkin bobbed his head dizzy in acquiescence, and Aunt Hannah Payne thought she was in church and shouted for joy.

The little town had awakened from its long post-bellum slumber and accepted with eagerness the upward impulse given it. It stood aside and looked on with something like adoration when Mr. Scatters and Mrs. Dunkin met and talked of ineffable things— things far above the ken of the average mortal.

When Mr. Scatters found that his mission was known, he gave up further attempts at concealing it and talked freely about the matter. He expatiated at length upon the responsibility that devolved upon him and his desire to discharge it, and he spoke glowingly of the great government whose power was represented by the seal which held the package of bonds. Not for one day would he stay away from his beloved Cuba, if it were not that that seal had to be broken in the presence of the proper authorities. So, however reluctant he might be to stay, it was not for him to shirk his task: he must wait for the sitting of court.

Meanwhile the Jacksons lived in an atmosphere of glory. The womenfolk purchased new dresses, and Isaac got a new wagon on the strength of their good fortune. It was nothing to what they dreamed of doing when they had the money positively in hand. Mr. Scatters still remained their guest, and they were proud of it.

What pleased them most was that their distinguished visitor seemed not to look down upon, but rather to be pleased with, their homely fare. Isaac had further cause for pleasure when his guest came to him later with a great show of frank confidence to request the loan of fifty dollars.

"I should not think of asking even this small favour of you but that I have only Cuban money with me and I knew you would feel distressed if you knew that I went to the trouble of sending this money away for exchange on account of so small a sum."

This was undoubtedly a mark of special confidence. It suddenly made Isaac feel as if the grand creature had accepted and labelled him as a brother and an equal. He hastened to Matthews' safe, where he kept his own earnings; for the grocer was banker as well.

With reverent hands they put aside the package of bonds and together counted out the required half a hundred dollars. In a little while Mr. Scatter's long, graceful fingers had closed over it.

Mr. Jackson's cup of joy was now full. It had but one bitter drop to mar its sweetness. That was the friendship that had sprung up between the Cuban and Mr. Dunkin. They frequently exchanged visits, and sat long together engaged in conversation from which Isaac was excluded. This galled him. He felt that he had a sort of proprietary interest in his guest. And any infringement of this property right he looked upon with distinct disfavour. So that it was with no pleasant countenance that he greeted Mr. Dunkin when he called on a certain night.

"Mr. Scatters is gone out," he said, as the old man entered and deposited his hat on the floor.

"Dat's all right, Isaac," said Mr. Dunkin slowly, "I didn't come to see de gent'man. I come to see you."

The cloud somewhat lifted from Isaac's brow. Mr. Dunkin was a man of importance and it made a deal of difference whom he was visiting.

He seemed a little bit embarrassed, however, as to how to open conversation. He hummed and hawed and was visibly uneasy. He tried to descant upon the weather, but the subject failed him. Finally, with an effort, he hitched his chair nearer to his host's and said in a low voice, "Ike, I reckon you has de confidence of Mistah Scatters?"

"I has," was the proud reply, "I has."

"Hum! uh! huh! Well—well—has you evah loant him any money?"

Isaac was aghast. Such impertinence!

"Mistah Dunkin," he began, "I considah——"

"Hol' on, Ike!" broke in Dunkin, laying a soothing hand on the other's knee, "don' git on yo' high hoss. Dis hyeah's a impo'tant mattah."

"I ain't got nothin' to say."

"He ain't never tol' you 'bout havin' nothin' but Cubian money on him?"

Isaac started.

"I see he have. He tol' me de same thing."

The two men sat staring suspiciously into each other's faces.

"He got a hun'ed an' fifty dollahs f'om me," said Dunkin.

"I let him have fifty," added Jackson weakly.

"He got a hun'ed an' fifty dollahs f'om thews. Dat's how I come to git 'spicious. He tol' him de same sto'y."

Again that pregnant look flashed between them, and they both rose and went out of the house.

They hurried down to Matthews' grocery. The owner was waiting for them there. There was solemnity, but no hesitation, in the manner with which they now went to the safe. They took out the package hastily and with ruthless hands. This was no ceremonial now. The seal had no longer any fears for them. They tore it off. They tore the wrappers. Then paper. Neatly folded paper. More wrapping paper. Newspapers. Nothing more. Of bills or bonds— nothing. With the debris of the mysterious parcel scattered about their feet, they stood up and looked at each other.

"I nevah did believe in furriners nohow," said Mr. Dunkin sadly.

"But he knowed all about my brothah John."

"An' he sho'ly did make mighty fine speeches. Maybe we's missed de money." This from the grocer.

Together they went over the papers again, with the same result.

"Do you know where he went to-night, Ike?"

"No."

"Den I reckon we's seed de las' o' him."

"But he lef' his valise."

"Yes, an' he lef' dis," said Dunkin sternly, pointing to the paper on the floor. "He sho'ly is mighty keerless of his valybles."

"Let's go git de constable," said the practical Matthews.

They did, though they felt that it would be unavailing.

The constable came and waited at Jackson's house. They had been there about half an hour, talking the matter over, when what was their surprise to hear Mr. Scatters' step coming jauntily up the walk. A sudden panic of terror and shame seized them. It was as if they had wronged him. Suppose, after all, everything should come right and he should be able to explain? They sat and trembled until he entered. Then the constable told him his mission.

Mr. Scatters was surprised. He was hurt. Indeed, he was distinctly grieved that his friends had had so little confidence in him. Had he been to them anything but a gentleman, a friend, and an honest man? Had he not come a long distance from his home to do one of them a favour? They hung their heads. Martha Ann, who was listening at the door, was sobbing audibly. What had he done thus to be humiliated? He saw the effect of his words and pursued it. Had he not left in the care of one of their own number security for his integrity in the shape of the bonds?

The effect of his words was magical. Every head went up and three pairs of flashing eyes were bent upon him. He saw and knew that they knew. He had not thought that they would dare to violate the seal around which he had woven such a halo. He saw that all was over, and, throwing up his hands with a despairing gesture, he bowed graciously and left the room with the constable.

All Miltonville had the story next day, and waited no less eagerly than before for the "settin' of co't."

To the anger and chagrin of Miltonvillians, Fox Run had the honour and distinction of being the county seat, and thither they must go to the sessions; but never did they so forget their animosities as on the day set for the trial of Scatters. They overlooked the pride of the Fox Runners, their cupidity and their vaunting arrogance. They ignored the indignity of showing interest in anything that took place in that village, and went in force, eager, anxious, and curious. Ahorse, afoot, by oxcart, by mule-wagon, white, black, high, low, old, and young of both sexes invaded Fox Run and swelled the crowd of onlookers until, with pity for the very anxiety of the people, the humane judge decided to discard the now inadequate court-room and hold the sessions on the village green. Here an impromptu bar was set up, and over against it were ranged the benches, chairs, and camp-stools of the spectators.

Every man of prominence in the county was present. Major Richardson, though now retired, occupied a distinguished position within the bar. Old Captain Howard shook hands familiarly with the judge and nodded to the assembly as though he himself had invited them all to be present. Former Judge Durbin sat with his successor on the bench.

Court opened and the first case was called. It gained but passing attention. There was bigger game to be stalked. A hog-stealing case fared a little better on account of the intimateness of the crime involved. But nothing was received with such awed silence as the case of the State against Joseph Scatters. The charge was obtaining money under false pretences, and the plea "Not Guilty."

The witnesses were called and their testimony taken. Mr. Scatters was called to testify in his own defence, but refused to do so. The prosecution stated its case and proceeded to sum up the depositions of the witnesses. As there was no attorney for the defence, the State's attorney delivered a short speech, in which the guilt of the defendant was plainly set forth. It was as clear as day. Things looked very dark for Mr. Scatters of Cuba.

As the lawyer sat down, and ere the case could be given to the jury, he rose and asked permission of the Court to say a few words.

This was granted him.

He stood up among them, a magnificent, strong, black figure. His eyes swept the assembly, judge, jury, and spectators with a look half amusement, half defiance.

"I have pleaded not guilty," he began in a low, distinct voice that could be heard in every part of the inclosure, "and I am not guilty of the spirit which is charged against me, however near the letter may touch me. I did use certain knowledge that I possessed, and the seal which I happened to have from an old government position, to defraud—that is the word, if you will—to defraud these men out of the price of their vanity and their cupidity. But it was not a long-premeditated thing. I was within a few miles of your town before the idea occurred to me. I was in straits. I stepped from the brink of great poverty into the midst of what you are pleased to deem a greater crime."

The Court held its breath. No such audacity had ever been witnessed in the life of Fox Run.

Scatters went on, warming to his subject as he progressed. He was eloquent and he was pleasing. A smile flickered over the face of Major Richardson and was reflected in the features of many others as the speaker burst forth:

"Gentlemen, I maintain that instead of imprisoning you should thank me for what I have done. Have I not taught your community a lesson? Have I not put a check upon their credulity and made them wary of unheralded strangers?"

He had. There was no disputing that. The judge himself was smiling, and the jurymen were nodding at each other.

Scatters had not yet played his trump card. He saw that the time was ripe. Straightening his form and raising his great voice, he cried: "Gentlemen, I am guilty according to the letter of the law, but from that I appeal to the men who make and have made the law. From the hard detail of this new day, I appeal to the chivalry of the old South which has been told in story and sung in song. From men of vindictiveness I appeal to men of mercy. From plebeians to aristocrats. By the memory of the sacred names of the Richardsons"—the Major sat bolt upright and dropped his snuff-box—"the Durbins"—the ex-judge couldn't for his life get his pince-nez on—"the Howards"—the captain openly rubbed his hands—"to the memory that those names call up I appeal, and to the living and honourable bearers of them present. And to you, gentlemen of the jury, the lives of whose fathers went to purchase this dark and bloody ground, I appeal from the accusation of these men, who are not my victims, not my dupes, but their own."

There was a hush when he was done. The judge read the charge to the jury, and it was favourable—very. And—well, Scatters had taught the darkies a lesson; he had spoken of their families and their traditions, he knew their names, and—oh, well, he was a good fellow after all—what was the use?

The jury did not leave their seats, and the verdict was acquittal.

Scatters thanked the Court and started away; but he met three ominous-looking pairs of eyes, and a crowd composed of angry Negroes was flocking toward the edge of the green.

He came back.

"I think I had better wait until the excitement subsides," he said to Major Richardson.

"No need of that, suh, no need of that. Here, Jim," he called to his coachman, "take Mr. Scatters wherever he wants to go, and remember, I shall hold you responsible for his safety."

"Yes, suh," said Jim.

"A thousand thanks, Major," said the man with the mission.

"Not at all, suh. By the way, that was a very fine effort of yours this afternoon. I was greatly moved by it. If you'll give me your address I'll send you a history of our family, suh, from the time they left Vuhginia and before."

Mr. Scatters gave him the address, and smiled at the three enemies, who still waited on the edge of the green.

"To the station," he said to the driver.

IV

A MATTER OF DOCTRINE

THERE WAS GREAT EXCITEMENT in Miltonville over the advent of a most eloquent and convincing minister from the North. The beauty about the Rev. Thaddeus Warwick was that he was purely and simply a man of the doctrine. He had no emotions, his sermons were never matters of feeling; but he insisted so strongly upon the constant presentation of the tenets of his creed that his presence in a town was always marked by the enthusiasm and joy of religious disputation.

The Rev. Jasper Hayward, coloured, was a man quite of another stripe. With him it was not so much what a man held as what he felt. The difference in their characteristics, however, did not prevent him from attending Dr. Warwick's series of sermons, where, from the vantage point of the gallery, he drank in, without assimilating, that divine's words of wisdom.

Especially was he edified on the night that his white brother held forth upon the doctrine of predestination. It was not that he understood it at all, but that it sounded well and the words had a rich ring as he champed over them again and again.

Mr. Hayward was a man for the time and knew that his congregation desired something new, and if he could supply it he was willing to take lessons even from a white co-worker who had neither "de spi'it ner de fiah." Because, as he was prone to admit to himself, "dey was sump'in' in de unnerstannin'."

He had no idea what plagiarism is, and without a single thought of wrong, he intended to reproduce for his people the religious wisdom which he acquired at the white church. He was an innocent beggar going to the doors of the well-provided for cold spiritual victuals to warm over for his own family. And it would not be

33

plagiarism either, for this very warming-over process would save it from that and make his own whatever he brought. He would season with the pepper of his homely wit, sprinkle it with the salt of his home-made philosophy, then, hot with the fire of his crude eloquence, serve to his people a dish his very own. But to the true purveyor of original dishes it is never pleasant to know that someone else holds the secret of the groundwork of his invention.

It was then something of a shock to the Reverend Mr. Hayward to be accosted by Isaac Middleton, one of his members, just as he was leaving the gallery on the night of this most edifying of sermons.

Isaac laid a hand upon his shoulder and smiled at him benevolently.

"How do, Brothah Hayward," he said, "you been sittin' unner de drippin's of de gospel, too?"

"Yes, I has been listenin' to de wo'ds of my fellow-laborah in de vineya'd of de Lawd," replied the preacher with some dignity, for he saw vanishing the vision of his own glory in a revivified sermon on predestination.

Isaac linked his arm familiarly in his pastor's as they went out upon the street.

"Well, what you t'ink erbout pre-o'dination an' fo'-destination any how?"

"It sutny has been pussented to us in a powahful light dis eve'nin'."

"Well, suh, hit opened up my eyes. I do' know when I's hyeahed a sehmon dat done my soul mo' good."

"It was a upliftin' episode."

"Seem lak 'co'din' to de way de brothah 'lucidated de matter to-night dat evaht'ing done sot out an' cut an' dried fu' us. Well dat's gwine to he'p me lots."

"De gospel is allus a he'p."

"But not allus in dis way. You see I ain't a eddicated man lak you, Brothah Hayward."

"We can't all have de same 'vantages," the preacher condescended. "But what I feels, I feels, an' what I unnerstan's, I unnerstan's. The Scripture tell us to get unnerstannin'."

"Well, dat's what I's been a-doin' to-night. I's been a-doubtin' an' a-doubtin', a-foolin' erroun' an' wonderin', but now I unnerstan'."

"'Splain yo'se'f, Brothah Middleton," said the preacher.

"Well, suh, I will to you. You knows Miss Sally Briggs? Huh, what say?"

The Reverend Hayward had given a half discernible start and an exclamation had fallen from his lips.

"What say?" repeated his companion.

"I knows de sistah ve'y well, she bein' a membah of my flock."

"Well, I been gwine in comp'ny wit dat ooman fu' de longes'. You ain't nevah tasted none o' huh cookin', has you?"

"I has 'sperienced de sistah's puffo'mances in dat line."

"She is the cookin'est ooman I evah seed in all my life, but how-somedever, I been gwine all dis time an' I ain' nevah said de wo'd. I nevah could git clean erway f'om huh widout somep'n' drawin' me back, an' I didn't know what hit was."

The preacher was restless.

"Hit was des dis away, Brothah Hayward, I was allus lingerin' on de brink, feahful to la'nch away, but now I's a-gwine to la'nch, case dat all dis time tain't been nuffin but fo'-destination dat been a-holdin' me on."

"Ahem," said the minister; "we mus' not be in too big a hu'y to put ouah human weaknesses upon some divine cause."

"I ain't a-doin' dat, dough I ain't a-sputin' dat de lady is a mos' oncommon fine lookin' pusson."

"I has only seed huh wid de eye of de spi'it," was the virtuous answer, "an' to dat eye all t'ings dat are good are beautiful."

"Yes, suh, an' lookin' wid de cookin' eye, hit seem lak' I des fo'destinated fu' to ma'y dat ooman."

"You say you ain't axe huh yit?"

"Not yit, but I's gwine to ez soon ez evah I gets de chanst now."

"Uh, huh," said the preacher, and he began to hasten his steps homeward.

"Seems lak you in a pow'ful hu'y to-night," said his companion, with some difficulty accommodating his own step to the preacher's masterly strides. He was a short man and his pastor was tall and gaunt.

"I has somp'n' on my min', Brothah Middleton, dat I wants to thrash out to-night in de sollertude of my own chambah," was the solemn reply.

"Well, I ain' gwine keep erlong wid you an' pestah you wid my chattah, Brothah Hayward," and at the next corner Isaac Middleton turned off and went his way, with a cheery "so long, may de Lawd set wid you in yo' meddertations."

"So long," said his pastor hastily. Then he did what would be strange in any man, but seemed stranger in so virtuous a minister. He checked his hasty pace, and, after furtively watching Middleton out of sight, turned and retraced his steps in a direction exactly opposite to the one in which he had been going, and toward the cottage of the very Sister Griggs concerning whose charms the minister's parishioner had held forth.

It was late, but the pastor knew that the woman whom he sought was industrious and often worked late, and with ever increasing eagerness he hurried on. He was fully rewarded for his perseverance when the light from the window of his intended hostess gleamed upon him, and when she stood in the full glow of it as the door opened in answer to his knock.

"La, Brothah Hayward, ef it ain't you; howdy; come in."

"Howdy, howdy, Sistah Griggs, how you come on?"

"Oh, I's des tol'able," industriously dusting a chair. "How's yo'se'f?"

"I's right smaht, thankee ma'am."

"W'y, Brothah Hayward, ain't you los' down in dis paht of de town?"

"No, indeed, Sistah Griggs, de shep'erd ain't nevah los' no whaih dey's any of de flock." Then looking around the room at the piles of ironed clothes, he added: "You sutny is a indust'ious ooman."

"I was des 'bout finishin' up some i'onin' I had fu' de white folks," smiled Sister Griggs, taking down her ironing-board and resting it in the corner. "Allus when I gits thoo my wo'k at nights I's putty well tiahed out an' has to eat a snack; set by, Brothah Hayward, while I fixes us a bite."

"La, sisteh, hit don't skacely seem right fu' me to be a-comin' in hyeah lettin' you fix fu' me at dis time o' night, an' you mighty nigh tuckahed out, too."

"Tsch, Brothah Hayward, taint no ha'dah lookin' out fu' two dan it is lookin' out fu' one."

Hayward flashed a quick upward glance at his hostess' face and then repeated slowly, "Yes'm, dat sutny is de trufe. I ain't nevah t'ought o' that befo'. Hit ain't no ha'dah lookin' out fu' two dan hit is fu' one," and though he was usually an incessant talker, he lapsed into a brown study.

Be it known that the Rev. Mr. Hayward was a man of a very level head, and that his bachelorhood was a matter of economy. He had long considered matrimony in the light of a most desirable estate, but one which he feared to embrace until the rewards for his labours began looking up a little better. But now the matter was being presented to him in an entirely different light. "Hit ain't no ha'dah lookin' out fu' two dan fu' one." Might that not be the truth after all. One had to have food. It would take very little more to do for two. One had to have a home to live in. The same house would shelter two. One had to wear clothes. Well, now, there came the rub. But he thought of donation parties, and smiled. Instead of being an extravagance, might not this union of two beings be an economy? Somebody to cook the food, somebody to keep the house, and somebody to mend the clothes.

His reverie was broken in upon by Sally Griggs' voice. "Hit do seem lak you mighty deep in t'ought dis evenin', Brothah Hayward. I done spoke to you twicet."

"Scuse me, Sistah Griggs, my min' has been mighty deeply 'sorbed in a little mattah o' doctrine. What you say to me?"

"I say set up to the table an' have a bite to eat; tain't much, but 'sich ez I have'—you know what de 'postle said."

The preacher's eyes glistened as they took in the well-filled board. There was fervour in the blessing which he asked that made amends for its brevity. Then he fell to.

Isaac Middleton was right. This woman was a genius among cooks. Isaac Middleton was also wrong. He, a layman, had no right to raise his eyes to her. She was the prize of the elect, not the quarry of any chance pursuer. As he ate and talked, his admiration for Sally grew as did his indignation at Middleton's presumption.

Meanwhile the fair one plied him with delicacies, and paid deferential attention whenever he opened his mouth to give vent to an opinion. An admirable wife she would make, indeed.

At last supper was over and his chair pushed back from the table. With a long sigh of content, he stretched his long legs, tilted back and said: "Well, you done settled de case ez fur ez I is concerned."

"What dat, Brothah Hayward?" she asked.

"Well, I do' know's I's quite prepahed to tell you yit."

"Hyeah now, don' you remembah ol' Mis' Eve? Taint nevah right to git a lady's cur'osity riz."

"Oh, nemmine, nemmine, I ain't gwine keep yo' cur'osity up long. You see, Sistah Griggs, you done 'lucidated one p'int to me dis night dat meks it plumb needful fu' me to speak."

She was looking at him with wide open eyes of expectation.

"You made de 'emark to-night, dat it ain't no ha'dah lookin' out aftah two dan one."

"Oh, Brothah Hayward!"

"Sistah Sally, I reckernizes dat, an' I want to know ef you won't let me look out aftah we two? Will you ma'y me?"

She picked nervously at her apron, and her eyes sought the floor modestly as she answered, "Why, Brothah Hayward, I ain't fittin' fu' no sich eddicated man ez you. S'posin' you'd git to be pu'sidin' elder, er bishop, er somp'n' er othah, whaih'd I be?"

He waved his hand magnanimously. "Sistah Griggs, Sally, whatevah high place I may be fo'destined to I shall tek my wife up wid me."

This was enough, and with her hearty yes, the Rev. Mr. Hayward had Sister Sally close in his clerical arms. They were not through their mutual felicitations, which were indeed so enthusiastic as to drown the sound of a knocking at the door and the ominous scraping of feet, when the door opened to admit Isaac Middleton, just as the preacher was imprinting a very decided kiss upon his fiancee's cheek.

"Wha'—wha'" exclaimed Middleton.

The preacher turned. "Dat you, Isaac?" he said complacently. "You must 'scuse ouah 'pearance, we des got ingaged."

The fair Sally blushed unseen.

"What!" cried Isaac. "Ingaged, aftah what I tol' you to-night." His face was a thundercloud.

"Yes, suh."

"An' is dat de way you stan' up fu' fo'destination?"

This time it was the preacher's turn to darken angrily as he replied, "Look a-hyeah, Ike Middleton, all I got to say to you is dat whenevah a lady cook to please me lak dis lady do, an' whenevah I love one lak I love huh, an' she seems to love me back, I's a-gwine to pop de question to huh, fo'destination er no fo'destination, so dah!"

The moment was pregnant with tragic possibilities. The lady still stood with bowed head, but her hand had stolen into her minister's. Isaac paused, and the situation overwhelmed him. Crushed with anger and defeat he turned toward the door.

On the threshold he paused again to say, "Well, all I got to say to you, Hayward, don' you nevah talk to me no mor' nuffin' 'bout doctrine!"

V

OLD ABE'S CONVERSION

THE NEGRO POPULATION of the little Southern town of Danvers was in a state of excitement such as it seldom reached except at revivals, baptisms, or on Emancipation Day. The cause of the commotion was the anticipated return of the Rev. Abram Dixon's only son, Robert, who, having taken up his father's life-work and graduated at one of the schools, had been called to a city church.

When Robert's ambition to take a college course first became the subject of the village gossip, some said that it was an attempt to force Providence. If Robert were called to preach, they said, he would be endowed with the power from on high, and no intervention of the schools was necessary. Abram Dixon himself had at first rather leaned to this side of the case. He had expressed his firm belief in the theory that if you opened your mouth, the Lord would fill it. As for him, he had no thought of what he should say to his people when he rose to speak. He trusted to the inspiration of the moment, and dashed blindly into speech, coherent or otherwise.

Himself a plantation exhorter of the ancient type, he had known no school except the fields where he had ploughed and sowed, the woods and the overhanging sky. He had sat under no teacher except the birds and the trees and the winds of heaven. If he did not fail utterly, if his labour was not without fruit, it was because he lived close to nature, and so, near to nature's God. With him religion was a matter of emotion, and he relied for his results more upon a command of feeling than upon an appeal to reason. So it was not strange that he should look upon his son's determination to learn to be a preacher as unjustified by the real demands of the ministry.

But as the boy had a will of his own and his father a boundless pride in him, the day came when, despite wagging heads, Robert Dixon went away to be enrolled among the students of a growing college. Since then six years had passed. Robert had spent his school vacations in teaching; and now, for the first time, he was coming home, a full-fledged minister of the gospel.

It was rather a shock to the old man's sensibilities that his son's congregation should give him a vacation, and that the young minister should accept; but he consented to regard it as of the new order of things, and was glad that he was to have his boy with him again, although he murmured to himself, as he read his son's letter through his bone-bowed spectacles: "Vacation, vacation, an' I wonder ef he reckons de devil's goin' to take one at de same time?"

It was a joyous meeting between father and son. The old man held his boy off and looked at him with proud eyes.

"Why, Robbie," he said, "you—you's a man!"

"That's what I'm trying to be, father." The young man's voice was deep, and comported well with his fine chest and broad shoulders.

"You's a bigger man den yo' father ever was!" said his mother admiringly.

"Oh, well, father never had the advantage of playing football."

The father turned on him aghast. "Playin' football!" he exclaimed. "You don't mean to tell me dat dey 'lowed men learnin' to be preachers to play sich games?"

"Oh, yes, they believe in a sound mind in a sound body, and one seems to be as necessary as the other in fighting evil."

Abram Dixon shook his head solemnly. The world was turning upside down for him.

"Football!" he muttered, as they sat down to supper.

Robert was sorry that he had spoken of the game, because he saw that it grieved his father. He had come intending to avoid rather than to combat his parent's prejudices. There was no condescension in his thought of them and their ways. They were different; that was all. He had learned new ways. They had retained the old. Even to himself he did not say, "But my way is the better one."

His father was very full of eager curiosity as to his son's conduct of his church, and the son was equally glad to talk of his work, for his whole soul was in it.

"We do a good deal in the way of charity work among the churchless and almost homeless city children; and, father, it would do your heart good if you could only see the little ones gathered together learning the first principles of decent living."

"Mebbe so," replied the father doubtfully, "but what you doin' in de way of teachin' dem to die decent?"

The son hesitated for a moment, and then he answered gently, "We think that one is the companion of the other, and that the best way to prepare them for the future is to keep them clean and good in the present."

"Do you give 'em good strong doctern, er do you give 'em milk and water?"

"I try to tell them the truth as I see it and believe it. I try to hold up before them the right and the good and the clean and beautiful."

"Humph!" exclaimed the old man, and a look of suspicion flashed across his dusky face. "I want you to preach fer me Sunday."

It was as if he had said, "I have no faith in your style of preaching the gospel. I am going to put you to the test."

Robert faltered. He knew his preaching would not please his father or his people, and he shrank from the ordeal. It seemed like setting them all at defiance and attempting to enforce his ideas over their own. Then a perception of his cowardice struck him, and he threw off the feeling that was possessing him. He looked up to find his father watching him keenly, and he remembered that he had not yet answered.

"I had not thought of preaching here," he said, "but I will relieve you if you wish it."

"De folks will want to hyeah you an' see what you kin do," pursued his father tactlessly. "You know dey was a lot of 'em dat said I oughtn't ha' let you go away to school. I hope you'll silence 'em."

Robert thought of the opposition his father's friends had shown to his ambitions, and his face grew hot at the memory. He felt his entire inability to please them now.

"I don't know, father, that I can silence those who opposed my going away or even please those who didn't, but I shall try to please One."

It was now Thursday evening, and he had until Saturday night to prepare his sermon. He knew Danvers, and remembered what a chill fell on its congregations, white or black, when a preacher appeared before them with a manuscript or notes. So, out of concession to their prejudices, he decided not to write his sermon, but to go through it carefully and get it well in hand. His work was often interfered with by the frequent summons to see old friends who stayed long, not talking much, but looking at him with some awe and a good deal of contempt. His trial was a little sorer than he had expected, but he bore it all with the good-natured philosophy which his school life and work in a city had taught him.

The Sunday dawned, a beautiful, Southern summer morning; the lazy hum of the bees and the scent of wild honeysuckle were in the air; the Sabbath was full of the quiet and peace of God; and yet the congregation which filled the little chapel at Danvers came with restless and turbulent hearts, and their faces said plainly: "Rob Dixon, we have not come here to listen to God's word. We have come here to put you on trial. Do you hear? On trial."

And the thought, "On trial," was ringing in the young minister's mind as he rose to speak to them. His sermon was a very quiet, practical one; a sermon that sought to bring religion before them as a matter of every-day life. It was altogether different from the torrent of speech that usually flowed from that pulpit. The people grew restless under this spiritual reserve. They wanted something to sanction, something to shout for, and here was this man talking to them as simply and quietly as if he were not in church.

As Uncle Isham Jones said, "De man never fetched an amen"; and the people resented his ineffectiveness. Even Robert's father sat with his head bowed in his hands, broken and ashamed of his son; and when, without a flourish, the preacher sat down, after talking twenty-two minutes by the clock, a shiver of surprise ran over the whole church. His father had never pounded the desk for less than an hour.

Disappointment, even disgust, was written on every face. The singing was spiritless, and as the people filed out of church and gathered in knots about the door, the old-time head-shaking was resumed, and the comments were many and unfavourable.

"Dat's what his schoolin' done fo' him," said one.

"It wasn't nothin' mo'n a lecter," was another's criticism.

"Put him 'side o' his father," said one of the Rev. Abram Dixon's loyal members, "and bless my soul, de ol' man would preach all roun' him, and he ain't been to no college, neither!"

Robert and his father walked home in silence together. When they were in the house, the old man turned to his son and said:

"Is dat de way dey teach you to preach at college?"

"I followed my instructions as nearly as possible, father."

"Well, Lawd he'p dey preachin', den! Why, befo' I'd ha' been in dat pulpit five minutes, I'd ha' had dem people moanin' an' hollerin' all over de church."

"And would they have lived any more cleanly the next day?"

The old man looked at his son sadly, and shook his head as at one of the unenlightened.

Robert did not preach in his father's church again before his visit came to a close; but before going he said, "I want you to promise me you'll come up and visit me, father. I want you to see the work I am trying to do. I don't say that my way is best or that my work is a higher work, but I do want you to see that I am in earnest."

"I ain't doubtin' you mean well, Robbie," said his father, "but I guess I'd be a good deal out o' place up thaih."

"No, you wouldn't, father. You come up and see me. Promise me."

And the old man promised.

It was not, however, until nearly a year later that the Rev. Abram Dixon went up to visit his son's church. Robert met him at the station, and took him to the little parsonage which the young clergyman's people had provided for him. It was a very simple place, and an aged woman served the young man as cook and caretaker; but Abram Dixon was astonished at what seemed to him both vainglory and extravagance.

"Ain't you livin' kin' o' high fo' yo' raisin', Robbie?" he asked.

The young man laughed. "If you'd see how some of the people live here, father, you'd hardly say so."

Abram looked at the chintz-covered sofa and shook his head at its luxury, but Robert, on coming back after a brief absence, found his father sound asleep upon the comfortable lounge.

On the next day they went out together to see something of the city. By the habit of years, Abram Dixon was an early riser, and his son was like him; so they were abroad somewhat before business was astir in the town. They walked through the commercial portion and down along the wharves and levees. On every side the same sight assailed their eyes: black boys of all ages and sizes, the waifs and strays of the city, lay stretched here and there on the wharves or curled on door-sills, stealing what sleep they could before the relentless day should drive them forth to beg a pittance for subsistence.

"Such as these we try to get into our flock and do something for," said Robert.

His father looked on sympathetically, and yet hardly with full understanding. There was poverty in his own little village, yes, even squalour, but he had never seen anything just like this. At home almost everyone found some open door, and rare was the wanderer who slept out-of-doors except from choice.

At nine o'clock they went to the police court, and the old minister saw many of his race appear as prisoners, receiving brief attention and long sentences. Finally a boy was arraigned for theft. He was a little, wobegone fellow hardly ten years of age. He was charged with stealing cakes from a bakery. The judge was about to deal with him as quickly as with the others, and Abram's heart bled for the child, when he saw a negro call the judge's attention. He turned to find that Robert had left his side. There was a whispered consultation, and then the old preacher heard with joy, "As this is his first offence and a trustworthy person comes forward to take charge of him, sentence upon the prisoner will be suspended."

Robert came back to his father holding the boy by the hand, and together they made their way from the crowded room.

"I'm so glad! I'm so glad!" said the old man brokenly.

"We often have to do this. We try to save them from the first contact with the prison and all that it means. There is no reformatory for black boys here, and they may not go to the institutions for the white; so for the slightest offence they are sent to jail, where they are placed with the most hardened criminals. When released they are branded forever, and their course is usually downward."

He spoke in a low voice, that what he said might not reach the ears of the little ragamuffin who trudged by his side.

Abram looked down on the child with a sympathetic heart.

"What made you steal dem cakes?" he asked kindly.

"I was hongry," was the simple reply.

The old man said no more until he had reached the parsonage, and then when he saw how the little fellow ate and how tenderly his son ministered to him, he murmured to himself, "Feed my lambs"; and then turning to his son, he said, "Robbie, dey's some'p'n in dis, dey's some'p'n in it, I tell you."

That night there was a boy's class in the lower room of Robert Dixon's little church. Boys of all sorts and conditions were there, and Abram listened as his son told them the old, sweet stories in the simplest possible manner and talked to them in his cheery, practical way. The old preacher looked into the eyes of the street gamins about him, and he began to wonder. Some of them were fierce, unruly-looking youngsters, inclined to meanness and rowdyism, but one and all, they seemed under the spell of their leader's voice. At last Robert said, "Boys, this is my father. He's a preacher, too. I want you to come up and shake hands with him." Then they crowded round the old man readily and heartily, and when they were outside the church, he heard them pause for a moment, and then three rousing cheers rang out with the vociferated explanation, "Fo' de minister's pap!"

Abram held his son's hand long that night, and looked with tear-dimmed eyes at the boy.

"I didn't understan'," he said. "I didn't understan'."

"You'll preach for me Sunday, father?"

"I wouldn't daih, honey. I wouldn't daih."

"Oh, yes, you will, pap."

He had not used the word for a long time, and at sound of it his father yielded.

It was a strange service that Sunday morning. The son introduced the father, and the father, looking at his son, who seemed so short a time ago unlearned in the ways of the world, gave as his text, "A little child shall lead them."

He spoke of his own conceit and vainglory, the pride of his age and experience, and then he told of the lesson he had learned. "Why, people," he said, "I feels like a new convert!"

It was a gentler gospel than he had ever preached before, and in the congregation there were many eyes as wet as his own.

"Robbie," he said, when the service was over, "I believe I had to come up here to be converted." And Robbie smiled.

VI

THE RACE QUESTION

SCENE—RACE TRACK. *Enter old coloured man, seating himself.*

"Oomph, oomph. De work of de devil sho' do p'ospah. How 'do, suh? Des tol'able, thankee, suh. How you come on? Oh, I was des a-sayin' how de wo'k of de ol' boy do p'ospah. Doesn't I frequent the racetrack? No, suh; no, suh. I's Baptis' myse'f, an' I 'low hit's all devil's doin's. Wouldn't 'a' be'n hyeah to-day, but I got a boy named Jim dat's long gone in sin an' he gwine ride one dem hosses. Oomph, dat boy! I sut'ny has talked to him and labohed wid him night an' day, but it was allers in vain, an' I's feahed dat de day of his reckonin' is at han'.

"Ain't I nevah been intrusted in racin'? Humph, you don't s'pose I been dead all my life, does you? What you laffin' at? Oh, scuse me, scuse me, you unnerstan' what I means. You don' give a ol' man time to splain hisse'f. What I means is dat dey has been days when I walked in de counsels of de on-gawdly and set in de seats of sinnahs; and long erbout dem times I did tek most ovahly strong to racin'.

"How long dat been? Oh, dat's way long back, 'fo' I got religion, mo'n thuty years ago, dough I got to own I has fell from grace several times sense.

"Yes, suh, I ust to ride. Ki-yi! I nevah furgit de day dat my ol' Mas' Jack put me on 'June Boy,' his black geldin', an' say to me, 'Si,' says he, 'if you don' ride de tail offen Cunnel Scott's mare, "No Quit," I's gwine to larrup you twell you cain't set in de saddle no mo'.' Hyah, hyah. My ol' Mas' was a mighty han' fu' a joke. I knowed he wan't gwine to do nuffin' to me.

"Did I win? Why, whut you spec' I's doin' hyeah ef I hadn' winned? W'y, ef I'd 'a' let dat Scott maih beat my 'June Boy' I'd 'a' drowned myse'f in Bull Skin Crick.

"Yes, suh, I winned; w'y, at de finish I come down dat track lak hit was de Jedgment Day an' I was de las' one up! Ef I didn't race dat maih's tail clean off, I 'low I made hit do a lot o' switchin'. An' aftah dat my wife Mandy she ma'ed me. Hyah, hyah, I ain't bin much on hol'in' de reins sence.

"Sh! dey comin' in to wa'm up. Dat Jim, dat Jim, dat my boy; you nasty putrid little rascal. Des a hundred an' eight, suh, des a hundred an' eight. Yas, suh, dat's my Jim; I don' know whaih he gits his dev'ment at.

"What's de mattah wid dat boy? Whyn't he hunch hisse'f up on dat saddle right? Jim, Jim, whyn't you limber up, boy; hunch yo'se'f up on dat hoss lak you belonged to him and knowed you was dah. What I done showed you? De black raskil, goin' out dah tryin' to disgrace his own daddy. Hyeah he come back. Dat's bettah, you scoun'ril.

"Dat's a right smaht-lookin' hoss he's a-ridin', but I ain't a-trustin' dat bay wid de white feet—dat is, not altogethah. She's a favourwright too; but dey's sumpin' else in dis worl' sides playin' favourwrights. Jim bettah had win dis race. His hoss ain't a five to one shot, but I spec's to go way fum hyeah wid money ernuff to mek a donation on de pa'sonage.

"Does I bet? Well, I don' des call hit bettin'; but I resks a little w'en I t'inks I kin he'p de cause. 'Tain't gamblin', o' co'se; I wouldn't gamble fu nothin', dough my ol' Mastah did ust to say dat a honest gamblah was ez good ez a hones' preachah an' mos' nigh ez skace.

"Look out dah, man, dey's off, dat nasty bay maih wid de white feet leadin' right fu'm de pos'. I knowed it! I knowed it! I had my eye on huh all de time. Oh, Jim, Jim, why didn't you git in bettah, way back dah fouf? Dah go de gong! I knowed dat wasn't no staht. Troop back dah, you raskils, hyah, hyah.

"I wush dat boy wouldn't do so much jummying erroun' wid dat hoss. Fust t'ing he know he ain't gwine to know whaih he's at.

"Dah, dah dey go ag'in. Hit's a sho' t'ing dis time. Bettah, Jim, bettah. Dey didn't leave you dis time. Hug dat bay mare, hug her close, boy. Don't press dat hoss yit. He holdin' back a lot o' t'ings.

"He's gainin'! doggone my cats, he's gainin'! an' dat hoss o' his'n gwine des ez stiddy ez a rockin'-chair. Jim allus was a good boy.

"Confound these spec's, I cain't see 'em skacely; huh, you say dey's neck an' neck; now I see 'em! now I see 'em! and Jimmy's a-ridin' like—— Huh, huh, I laik to said sumpin'.

"De bay maih's done huh bes', she's done huh bes'! Dey's turned into the stretch an' still see-sawin'. Let him out, Jimmy, let him out! Dat boy done th'owed de reins away. Come on, Jimmy, come on! He's leadin' by a nose. Come on, I tell you, you black rapscallion, come on! Give 'em hell, Jimmy! give 'em hell! Under de wire an' a len'th ahead. Doggone my cats! wake me up w'en dat othah hoss comes in.

"No, suh, I ain't gwine stay no longah, I don't app'ove o' racin', I's gwine 'roun' an' see dis hyeah bookmakah an' den I's gwine dreckly home, suh, dreckly home. I's Baptis' myse'f, an' I don't app'ove o' no sich doin's!"

VII

A DEFENDER OF THE FAITH

THERE WAS A VERY ANIMATED discussion going on, on the lower floor of the house Number Ten "D" Street. House Number Ten was the middle one of a row of more frames, which formed what was put down on the real estate agent's list as a coloured neighbourhood. The inhabitants of the little cottages were people so poor that they were constantly staggering on the verge of the abyss, which they had been taught to dread and scorn, and why, clearly. Life with them was no dream, but a hard, terrible reality, which meant increasing struggle, and little wonder then that the children of such parents should see the day before Christmas come without hope of any holiday cheer.

Christmas; what did it mean to them? The pitiful little dark ragmuffins, save that the happy, well-dressed people who passed the shanties seemed further away from their life, save that mother toiled later in the evening at her work, if there was work, and that father drank more gin and prayed louder in consequence; save that, perhaps—and there was always a donation—that there might be a little increase in the amount of cold victuals that big sister brought home, and there might be turkey-dressing in it.

But there was a warm discussion in Number Ten, and that is the principal thing. The next in importance is that Miss Arabella Coe, reporter, who had been down that way looking mainly for a Christmas story, heard the sound of voices raised in debate, and paused to listen. It was not a very polite thing for Miss Coe to do, but then Miss Coe was a reporter and reporters are not scrupulous about being polite when there is anything to hear. Besides, the pitch to which the lusty young voices within were raised argued that the owners did not care if the outside world shared in the

49

conversation. So Arabella listened, and after a while she passed through the gate and peeped into the room between the broken slats of a shutter.

It was a mean little place, quite what might be expected from its exterior. A cook stove sat in the middle of the floor with a smoky fire in it, and about it were clustered four or five black children ranging from a toddler of two to a boy of ten. They all showed differing degrees of dirt and raggedness, but all were far and beyond the point of respectability.

One of the group, the older boy, sat upon the bed and was holding forth to his brothers and sisters not without many murmurs of doubt and disbelief.

"No," he was saying, "I tell you dey hain't no such thing as a Santy Claus. Dat's somep'n dat yo' folks jes' git up to make you be good long 'bout Christmas time. I know."

"But, Tom, you know what mammy said," said a dreamy-eyed little chap, who sat on a broken stool with his chin on his hands.

"Aw, mammy," said the orator, "she's jes' a-stuffin' you. She don' believe in no Santy Claus hersel', less'n why'nt he bring huh de dress she prayed fu' last Christmas." He was very wise, this old man of ten years, and he had sold papers on the avenue where many things are learned, both good and bad.

"But what you got to say about pappy?" pursued the believer. "He say dey's a Santy Claus, and dat he comes down de chimbly; and———"

"Whut's de mattah wid you; look at dat stove pipe; how you s'pose anybody go'n' to git in hyeah th'oo de chimbly?"

They all looked up at the narrow, rusty stove pipe and the sigh of hopelessness brought the tears to Arabella's eyes. The children seemed utterly nonplussed, and Tom was swelling at his triumph. "How's any Santy Claus go'n' to come down th'oo that, I want to know," he repeated.

But the faith of childhood is stronger than reason. Tom's little sister piped up, "I don't know how, but he comes th'roo' that away anyhow. He brung Mamie Davith a doll and it had thoot on it out o' the chimbly."

It was now Tom's turn to be stumped, but he wouldn't let it be known. He only said, "Aw," contemptuously and coughed for more crushing arguments.

"I knows dey's a Santy Claus," said dreamy-eyed Sam.

"Ef dey is why'n't he never come here?" retorted Tom.

"I jes' been thinkin' maybe ouah house is so little he miss it in de night; dey says he's a ol' man an' I 'low his sight ain' good."

Tom was stricken into silence for a moment by this entirely new view of the matter, and then finding no answer to it, he said "Aw" again and looked superior, but warningly so

"Maybe Thanty's white an' don' go to see col'red people," said the little girl.

"But I do know coloured people's houses he's been at," contended Sam. "Aw, dem col'red folks dat's got the money, dem's de only ones dat Santy Claus fin's, you bet."

Arabella at the window shuddered at the tone of the sceptic; it reminded her so much of the world she knew, and it was hard to believe that her friends who prided themselves on their unbelief could have anything in common with a little coloured newsboy down on "D" Street.

"Tell you what," said Sam again, "let's try an' see if dey is a Santy. We'll put a light in the winder, so if he's ol' he can see us anyhow, an' we'll pray right hard fu' him to come."

"Aw," said Tom.

"Ith been good all thish month," chirped the little girl.

The other children joined with enthusiasm in Sam's plan, though Tom sat upon the bed and looked scornfully on.

Arabella escaped from the window just as Sam brought the smoky lamp and set it on the sill, but she still stood outside the palings of the fence and looked in. She saw four little forms get down on their knees and she crept up near again to hear.

Following Sam's lead they began, "Oh, Santy," but Tom's voice broke in, "Don't you know the Lord don't 'low you to pray to nobody but Him?"

Sam paused, puzzled for a minute, then he led on: "Please 'scuse, good Lord, we started wrong, but won't you please, sir, send Santy Clause around. Amen." And they got up from their knees satisfied.

"Aw," said Tom as Arabella was turning wet-eyed away.

It was a good thing the reporter left as soon as she did, for in a few minutes a big woman pushed in at the gate and entered the house.

"Mammy, mammy," shrieked the children.

."Lawsy, me," said Martha, laughing, "who evah did see sich children? Bless dey hearts, an' dey done sot dey lamp in de winder, too, so's dey po' ol' mammy kin see to git in."

As she spoke she was taking the lamp away to set it on the table where she had placed her basket, but the cry of the children stopped her. "Oh, no, mammy, don't take it, don't take it, dat's to light Santy Claus in."

She paused a minute bewildered and then the light broke over her face. She smiled and then a rush of tears quenched the smile. She gathered the children into her arms and said, "I's feared, honey, ol' man Santy ain' gwine fu' you to-night."

"Wah'd I tell you?" sneered Tom.

"You hush yo' mouf," said his mother, and she left the lamp where it was.

As Arabella Coe wended her way home that night her brain was busy with many thoughts. "I've got my story at last," she told herself, "and I'll go on up and write it." But she did not go up to write it. She came to the parting of the ways. One led home, the other to the newspaper office where she worked. She laughed nervously, and took the former way. Once in her room she went through her small store of savings. There was very little there, then she looked down ruefully at her worn boots. She did need a new pair. Then, holding her money in her hand, she sat down to think.

"It's really a shame," she said to herself, "those children will have no Christmas at all, and they'll never believe in Santa Claus again. They will lose their faith forever and from this it will go to other things." She sat there dreaming for a long while and the vision of a very different childhood came before her eyes.

"Dear old place," she murmured softly, "I believed in Santa Claus until I was thirteen, and that oldest boy is scarcely ten." Suddenly she sprung to her feet. "Hooray," she cried, "I'll be defender of the faith," and she went out into the lighted streets again.

The shopkeepers looked queerly at Arabella that night as she bought as if she were the mother of a large and growing family, and she appeared too young for that. Finally, there was a dress for mother.

She carried them down on "D" Street and placed them stealthily at the door of Number Ten. She put a note among the things, which read: "I am getting old and didn't see your house last year, also I am getting fat and couldn't get down that little stove pipe of yours this year. You must excuse me. Santa Claus." Then looking wilfully at her shoes, but nevertheless with a glow on her face, she went up to the office to write her story.

There were joyous times at Number Ten the next day. Mother was really surprised, and the children saw it.

"Wha'd I tell you," said dreamy Sam.

Tom said nothing then, but when he went down to the avenue to sell the morning papers, all resplendent in a new muffler, he strode up to a boy and remarked belligerently, "Say, if you says de ain't no Santy Claus again, I'll punch yo' head."

VIII

CAHOOTS

IN THE CENTRE of the quaint old Virginia grave-yard stood two monuments side by side—two plain granite shafts exactly alike. On one was inscribed the name Robert Vaughan Fairfax and the year 1864. On the other was the simple and perplexing inscription, "Cahoots." Nothing more.

The place had been the orchard of one of the ante-bellum mansions before the dead that were brought back from the terrible field of Malvern Hill and laid there had given it a start as a cemetery. Many familiar names were chiselled on the granite head-stones, and anyone conversant with Virginia genealogy would have known them to belong to some of the best families of the Old Dominion. But "Cahoots,"—who or what was he?

My interest, not to say curiosity, was aroused. There must be a whole story in those two shafts with their simple inscriptions, a life-drama or perhaps a tragedy. And who was more likely to know it than the postmaster of the quaint little old town. Just after the war, as if tired with its exertions to repel the invader, the old place had fallen asleep and was still drowsing.

I left the cemetery—if such it could be called—and wended my way up the main street to the ancient building which did duty as post-office. The man in charge, a grizzled old fellow with an empty sleeve, sat behind a small screen. He looked up as I entered and put out his hand toward the mailboxes, waiting for me to mention my name. But instead I said: "I am not expecting any mail. I only wanted to ask a few questions."

"Well, sir, what can I do for you?" he asked with some interest.

"I've just been up there walking through the cemetery," I

returned, "and I am anxious to know the story, if there be one, of two monuments which I saw there."

"You mean Fairfax and Cahoots."

"Yes."

"You're a stranger about here, of course."

"Yes," I said again, "and so there is a story?"

"There is a story and I'll tell it to you. Come in and sit down." He opened a wire door into his little cage, and I seated myself on a stool and gave my attention to him.

"It's just such a story," he began, "as you can hear in any of the Southern States—wherever there were good masters and faithful slaves. This particular tale is a part of our county history, and there ain't one of the old residents but could tell it to you word for word and fact for fact. In the days before our misunderstanding with the North, the Fairfaxes were the leading people in this section. By leading, I mean not only the wealthiest, not only the biggest land-owners, but that their name counted for more in social circles and political councils than any other hereabout. It is natural to expect that such a family should wish to preserve its own name down a direct line. So it was a source of great grief to old Fairfax that his first three children were girls, pretty, healthy, plump enough little things, but girls for all that, and consequently a disappointment to their father's pride of family. When the fourth child came and it proved to be a boy, the Fairfax plantation couldn't hold the Fairfax joy and it flowed out and mellowed the whole county.

"They do say that Fairfax Fairfax was in one of his further tobacco fields when the good news was brought to him, and that after giving orders that all the darkies should knock off work and take a holiday, in his haste and excitement he jumped down from his horse and ran all the way to the house. I give the story only for what it is worth. But if it is true, it is the first case of a man of that name and family forgetting himself in an emergency.

"Well, of course, the advent of a young male Fairfax would under any circumstances have proven a great event, although it was afterwards duplicated, but there would have been no story to tell, there would have been no 'Cahoots,' if by some fortuitous circumstance one of the slave women had not happened to bring into the world that day and almost at the same time that her mistress was introducing young Vaughan Fairfax to the light, a little black pickaninny of her own. Well, if you're a Southern man, and I take it that you are, you know that nothing ever happens in the quarters that the big house doesn't know. So the news was soon at the white father's ears and nothing would do him but that the black baby must be brought to the house and be introduced to the white one. The little black fellow came in all rolled in his bundle of shawls and was laid for a few minutes beside his little lord and master. Side by side they lay blinking at the light equally strange to both, and then the master took the black child's hand and put it in that of the white's. With the convulsive gesture common to babyhood the little hands clutched in a feeble grasp.

"'Dah now,' old Doshy said—she was the nurse that had brought the pickaninny up—'dey done tol' each othah howdy.'

"'Told each other howdy nothing,' said old Fairfax solemnly, 'they have made a silent compact of eternal friendship, and I propose to ratify it right here.'

"He was a religious man, and so there with all the darkies clustered around in superstitious awe, and with the white face of his wife looking at him from among the pillows, he knelt and offered a prayer, and asked a blessing upon the two children just come into the world. And through it all those diminutive specimens of humanity lay there blinking with their hands still clasped.

"Well, they named the white child Robert Vaughan, and they began calling the little darky Ben, until an incident in later life gave him the name that clung to him till the last, and which the Fairfaxes have had chiseled on his tomb-stone.

"The incident occurred when the two boys were about five years old. They were as thick as thieves, and two greater scamps and greater cronies never tramped together over a Virginia plantation. In the matter of deviltry they were remarkably precocious, and it was really wonderful what an amount of mischief those two could do. As was natural, the white boy planned the deeds, and the black one was his willing coadjutor in carrying them out.

Meanwhile, the proud father was smilingly indulgent to their pranks, but even with him the climax was reached when one of his fine young hounds was nearly driven into fits by the clatter of a tin can tied to its tail. Then the two culprits were summoned to appear before the paternal court of inquiry.

"They came hand in hand, and with no great show of fear or embarrassment. They had gotten off so many times before that they were perfectly confident of their power in this case to cajole the judge. But to their surprise he was all sternness and severity.

"'Now look here,' he said, after expatiating on the cruel treatment which the dog had received. 'I want to know which one of you tied the can to Spot's tail?'

"Robert Vaughan looked at Ben, and Ben looked back at him. Silence there, and nothing more.

"'Do you hear my question?' old Fairfax asked with rising voice.

"Robert Vaughan looked straight ahead of him, and Ben dug his big toe into the sand at the foot of the veranda, but neither answered.

"'Robert Vaughan Fairfax,' said his father, 'who played that trick on Spot? Answer me, do you hear?'

"The Fairfax heir seemed suddenly to have grown deaf and dumb, and the father turned to the black boy. His voice took on the tone of command which he had hardly used to his son. 'Who played that trick on Spot? Answer me, Ben.'

"The little darky dug harder and harder into the sand, and flashed a furtive glance from under his brows at his fellow-conspirator. Then he drawled out, 'I done it.'

"'You didn't,' came back the instant retort from his young master, 'I did it myself.'

"'I done it,' repeated Ben, and 'You didn't,' reiterated his young master.

"The father sat and looked on at the dispute, and his mouth twitched suspiciously, but he spoke up sternly. 'Well, if I can't get the truth out of you this way, I'll try some other plan. Mandy,' he hailed a servant, 'put these boys on a diet of bread and water until they are ready to answer my questions truthfully.'

"The culprits were led away to their punishment. Of course it would have just been meat to Mandy to have stolen something to the youngsters, but her master kept such a close eye upon her that she couldn't, and when brought back at the end of three hours, their fare had left the prisoners rather hungry. But they had evidently disputed the matter between themselves, and from the cloud on their faces when they reappeared before their stern judge, it was still unsettled.

"To the repetition of the question, Vaughan answered again, 'I did it,' and then his father tried Ben again.

"After several efforts, and an imploring glance at his boy master, the little black stammered out:

"'Well, I reckon—I reckon, Mas,' me an' Mas' Vaughan, we done it in cahoots.'

"Old Fairfax Fairfax had a keen sense of humour, and as he looked down on the strangely old young darky and took in his answer, the circumstance became too much for his gravity, and his relaxing laugh sent the culprits rolling and tumbling in the sand in an ectasy of relief from the strained situation.

"'Cahoots—I reckon it was "Cahoots,"' the judge said. 'You ought to be named that, you little black rascal!' Well, the story got around, and so it was, and from that day forth the black boy was 'Cahoots.' Cahoots, whether on the plantation, at home, in the halls of the Northern College, where he accompanied his young master, or in the tragic moments of the great war-drama played out on the field of Malvern.

"As they were in childhood, so, inseparable through youth and young manhood, Robert Fairfax and Cahoots grew up. They were together in everything, and when the call came that summoned the young Virginian from his college to fight for the banner of his State, Cahoots was the one who changed from the ease of a gentleman's valet to the hardship of a soldier's body-servant.

"The last words Fairfax Fairfax said as his son cantered away in his gray suit were addressed to Cahoots: 'Take good care of your Mas' Vaughan, Cahoots, and don't come back without him.'

"'I won't, Mastah,' Cahoots flung back and galloped after his life-long companion.

"Well, the war brought hard times both for master and man, and there were no flowery beds of ease even for the officers who wore the gray. Robert Fairfax took the fortunes of the conflict like a man and a Virginia gentleman, and with him Cahoots.

"It was at Malvern Hill that the young Confederate led his troops into battle, and all day long the booming of the cannon and the crash of musketry rising above the cries of the wounded and dying came to the ears of the slave waiting in his tent for his master's return. Then in the afternoon a scattered fragment came straggling back into the camp. Cahoots went out to meet them. The firing still went on.

"'Whah's Mas' Bob?' his voice pierced through the cannon's thunder.

"'He fell at the front, early in the battle.'"

"'Whah's his body den, ef he fell?'

"'We didn't have time to look for dead bodies in that murderous fire. It was all we could do to get our living bodies away.'

"'But I promised not to go back without him.' It was a wail of anguish from the slave.

"'Well, you'll have to.'

"'I won't. Whah did he fall?'

"Someone sketched briefly the approximate locality of Robert Fairfax's resting place, and on the final word Cahoots tore away.

"The merciless shot of the Federals was still raking the field. But amid it all an old prairie schooner, gotten from God knows where, started out from the dismantled camp across the field. 'Some fool going to his death,' said one of the gray soldiers.

"A ragged, tattered remnant of the wagon came back. The horses were bleeding and staggering in their steps. The very harness was cut by the balls that had grazed it. But with a light in his eyes and the look of a hero, Cahoots leaped from the tattered vehicle and began dragging out the body of his master.

"He had found him far to the front in an abandoned position and brought him back over the field of the dead.

"'How did you do it?' They asked him.

"'I jes' had to do it,' he said. 'I promised not to go home widout him, and I didn't keer ef I did git killed. I wanted to die ef I couldn't find Mas' Bob's body.'

"He carried the body home, and mourned at the burial, and a year later came back to the regiment with the son who had come after Robert, and was now just of fighting age. He went all through this campaign, and when the war was over, the two struck away into the mountains. They came back after a while, neither one having taken the oath of allegiance, and if there were any rebels Cahoots was as great a one to the day of his death as his master. That tomb-stone, you see it looks old, was placed there at the old master's request when his dead son came home from Malvern Hill, for he said when Cahoots went to the other side they must not be separated; that accounts for its look of age, but it was not until last year that we laid Cahoots—Cahoots still though an old man—beside his master. And many a man that had owned his people, and many another that had fought to continue that ownership, dropped a tear on his grave."

IX

THE PROMOTER

EVEN AS EARLY AS SEPTEMBER, in the year of 1870, the newly eman-
cipated had awakened to the perception of the commercial advan-
tages of freedom, and had begun to lay snares to catch the fleet and
elusive dollar. Those controversialists who say that the Negro's only
idea of freedom was to live without work are either wrong, mali-
cious, or they did not know Little Africa when the boom was on;
when every little African, fresh from the fields and cabins, dreamed
only of untold wealth and of mansions in which he would have
been thoroughly uncomfortable. These were the devil's sunny days,
and early and late his mowers were in the field. These were the days
of benefit societies that only benefited the shrewdest man; of
mutual insurance associations, of wild building companies, and of
gilt-edged land schemes wherein the unwary became bogged. This
also was the day of Mr. Jason Buford, who, having been free before
the war, knew a thing or two, and now had set himself up as a
promoter. Truly he had profited by the example of the white men
for whom he had so long acted as messenger and factotum.

As he frequently remarked when for purposes of business he
wished to air his Biblical knowledge, "I jest takes the Scripter fur
my motter an' foller that ol' passage where it says, 'Make hay while
the sun shines, fur the night cometh when no man kin work.'"

It is related that one of Mr. Buford's customers was an old plantation exhorter. At the first suggestion of a Biblical quotation the
old gentleman closed his eyes and got ready with his best amen. But
as the import of the words dawned on him he opened his eyes in
surprise, and the amen died a-borning. "But do hit say dat?" he
asked earnestly.

"It certainly does read that way," said the promoter glibly.

"Uh, huh," replied the old man, settling himself back in his chair. "I been preachin' dat t'ing wrong fu' mo' dan fo'ty yeahs. Dat's whut comes o' not bein' able to read de wo'd fu' yo'se'f."

Buford had no sense of the pathetic or he could never have done what he did—sell to the old gentleman, on the strength of the knowledge he had imparted to him, a house and lot upon terms so easy that he might drowse along for a little time and then wake to find himself both homeless and penniless. This was the promoter's method, and for so long a time had it proved successful that he had now grown mildly affluent and had set up a buggy in which to drive about and see his numerous purchasers and tenants.

Buford was a suave little yellow fellow, with a manner that suggested the training of some old Southern butler father, or at least, an experience as a likely house-boy. He was polite, plausible, and more than all, resourceful. All of this he had been for years, but in all these years he had never so risen to the height of his own uniqueness as when he conceived and carried into execution the idea of the "Buford Colonizing Company."

Humanity has always been looking for an Eldorado, and, however mixed the metaphor may be, has been searching for a Moses to lead it thereto. Behold, then, Jason Buford in the rôle of Moses. And equipped he was to carry off his part with the very best advantage, for though he might not bring water from the rock, he could come as near as any other man to getting blood from a turnip.

The beauty of the man's scheme was that no offering was too small to be accepted. Indeed, all was fish that came to his net.

Think of paying fifty cents down and knowing that some time in the dim future you would be the owner of property in the very heart of a great city where people would rush to buy. It was glowing enough to attract a people more worldly wise than were these late slaves. They simply fell into the scheme with all their souls; and off their half dollars, dollars, and larger sums, Mr. Buford waxed opulent. The land meanwhile did not materialise.

It was just at this time that Sister Jane Callender came upon the scene and made glad the heart of the new-fledged Moses. He had heard of Sister Jane before, and he had greeted her coming with a sparkling of eyes and a rubbing of hands that betokened a joy with a good financial basis.

The truth about the newcomer was that she had just about received her pension, or that due to her deceased husband, and she would therefore be rich, rich to the point where avarice would lie in wait for her.

Sis' Jane settled in Mr. Buford's bailiwick, joined the church he attended, and seemed only waiting with her dollars for the very call which he was destined to make. She was hardly settled in a little three-room cottage before he hastened to her side, kindly intent, or its counterfeit, beaming from his features. He found a weak-looking old lady propped in a great chair, while another stout and healthy-looking woman ministered to her wants or stewed about the house in order to be doing something.

"Ah, which—which is Sis' Jane Callender," he asked, rubbing his hands for all the would like a clothing dealer over a good customer.

"Dat's Sis' Jane in de cheer," said the animated one, pointing to her charge. "She feelin' mighty po'ly dis evenin'. What might be yo' name?" She was promptly told.

"Sis' Jane, hyeah one de good brothahs come to see you to offah his suvices if you need anything."

"Thanky, brothah, charity," said the weak voice, "sit yo'se'f down. You set down, Aunt Dicey. Tain't no use a runnin' roun' waitin' on me. I ain't long fu' dis worl' nohow, mistah."

"Buford is my name an' I came in to see if I could be of any assistance to you, a-fixin' up yo' mattahs er seein' to anything for you."

"Hit's mighty kind o' you to come, dough I don' 'low I'll need much fixin' fu' now."

"Oh, we hope you'll soon be better, Sistah Callender."

"Nevah no mo', suh, 'til I reach the Kingdom."

"Sis' Jane Callender, she have been mighty sick," broke in Aunt Dicey Fairfax, "but I reckon she gwine pull thoo', the Lawd willin'."

"Amen," said Mr. Buford.

"Huh, uh, children, I done hyeahd de washin' of de waters of Jerdon."

"No, no, Sistah Callendah, we hope to see you well and happy in de injoyment of de pension dat I understan' de gov'ment is goin' to give you."

"La, chile, I reckon de white folks gwine to git dat money. I ain't nevah gwine to live to 'ceive it. Des' aftah I been wo'kin' so long fu' it, too."

The small eyes of Mr. Buford glittered with anxiety and avarice. What, was this rich plum about to slip from his grasp, just as he was about to pluck it? It should not be. He leaned over the old lady with intense eagerness in his gaze.

"You must live to receive it," he said, "we need that money for the race. It must not go back to the white folks. Ain' you got nobody to leave it to?"

"Not a chick ner a chile, 'ceptin' Sis' Dicey Fairfax here."

Mr. Buford breathed again. "Then leave it to her, by all means," he said.

"I don' want to have nothin' to do with de money of de daid," said Sis' Dicey Fairfax.

"Now, don't talk dat away, Sis' Dicey," said the sick woman. "Brother Buford is right, case you sut'ny has been good to me sence I been layin' hyeah on de bed of affliction, an' dey ain't nobody more fitterner to have dat money den you is. Ef de Lawd des lets me live long enough, I's gwine to mek my will in yo' favoh."

"De Lawd's will be done," replied the other with resignation, and Mr. Buford echoed with an "Amen!"

He stayed very long that evening, planning and talking with the two old women, who received his words as the Gospel. Two weeks later the *Ethiopian Banner,* which was the organ of Little Africa, announced that Sis' Jane Callender had received a back pension which amounted to more than five hundred dollars. Thereafter Mr. Buford was seen frequently in the little cottage, until one day, after a lapse of three or four weeks, a policeman entered Sis' Jane Callender's cottage and led her away amidst great excitement to prison. She was charged with pension fraud, and against her protestations, was locked up to await the action of the Grand Jury.

The promoter was very active in his client's behalf, but in spite of all his efforts she was indicted and came up for trial.

It was a great day for the denizens of Little Africa, and they crowded the court room to look upon this stranger who had come among them to grow so rich, and then suddenly to fall so low.

The prosecuting attorney was a young Southerner, and when he saw the prisoner at the bar he started violently, but checked himself. When the prisoner saw him, however, she made no effort at self control.

"Lawd o' mussy," she cried, spreading out her black arms, "if it ain't Miss Lou's little Bobby."

The judge checked the hilarity of the audience; the prosecutor maintained his dignity by main force, and the bailiff succeeded in keeping the old lady in her place, although she admonished him: "Pshaw, chile, you needn't fool wid me, I nussed dat boy's mammy when she borned him."

It was too much for the young attorney, and he would have been less a man if it had not been. He came over and shook her hand warmly, and this time no one laughed.

It was really not worth while prolonging the case, and the prosecution was nervous. The way that old black woman took the court and its officers into her bosom was enough to disconcert any ordinary tribunal. She patronised the judge openly before the hearing began and insisted upon holding a gentle motherly conversation with the foreman of the jury.

She was called to the stand as the very first witness.

"What is your name?" asked the attorney.

"Now, Bobby, what is you axin' me dat fu'? You know what my name is, and you one of de Fairfax fambly, too. I 'low ef yo' mammy was hyeah, she'd mek you 'membah; she'd put you in yo' place."

The judge rapped for order.

"That is just a manner of proceeding," he said; "you must answer the question, so the rest of the court may know."

"Oh, yes, suh, 'scuse me, my name hit's Dicey Fairfax."

The attorney for the defence threw up his hands and turned purple. He had a dozen witnesses there to prove that they had known the woman as Jane Callender.

"But did you not give your name as Jane Callender?"

"I object," thundered the defence.

"Do, hush, man," Sis' Dicey exclaimed, and then turning to the prosecutor, "La, honey, you know Jane Callender ain't my real name, you knows dat yo'se'f. It's des my bus'ness name. W'y, Sis' Jane Callender done daid an' gone to glory too long 'go fu' to talk erbout."

"Then you admit to the court that your name is not Jane Callender?"

"Wha's de use o' my 'mittin', don' you know it yo'se'f, suh? Has I got to come hyeah at dis late day an' p'ove my name an' redentify befo' my ol' Miss's own chile? Mas' Bob, I nevah did t'ink you'd ac' dat away. Freedom sutny has done tuk erway yo' mannahs."

"Yes, yes, yes, that's all right, but we want to establish the fact that your name is Dicey Fairfax."

"Cose it is."

"Your Honor, I object —I————"

"Your Honor," said Fairfax coldly, "will you grant me the liberty of conducting the examination in a way somewhat out of the ordinary lines? I believe that my brother for the defence will have nothing to complain of. I believe that I understand the situation and shall be able to get the truth more easily by employing methods that are not altogether technical."

The court seemed to understand a thing or two himself, and overruled the defence's objection.

"Now, Mrs. Fairfax————"

Aunt Dicey snorted. "Hoomph? What? Mis' Fairfax? What ou say, Bobby Fairfax? What you call me dat fu'? My name Aunt Dicey to you an' I want you to un'erstan' dat right hyeah. Ef you keep on foolin' wid me, I 'spec' my patience gwine waih claih out."

"Excuse me. Well, Aunt Dicey, why did you take the name of Jane Callender if your name is really Dicey Fairfax?"

"W'y, I done tol' you, Bobby, dat Sis' Jane Callender was des' my bus'ness name."

"Well, how were you to use this business name?"

"Well, it was des dis away. Sis' Jane Callender, she gwine git huh pension, but la, chile, she tuk down sick unto deaf, an' Brothah Buford, he say dat she ought to mek a will in favoh of somebody, so's de money would stay 'mongst ouah folks, an' so, bimeby, she 'greed she mek a will."

"And who is Brother Buford, Aunt Dicey?"

"Brothah Buford? Oh, he's de gemman whut come an' offered to 'ten' to Sis' Jane Callender's bus'ness fu' huh. He's a moughty clevah man."

"And he told her she ought to make a will?"

"Yas, suh. So she 'greed she gwine mek a will, an' she say to me, 'Sis Dicey, you sut'ny has been good to me sence I been layin' hyeah on dis bed of 'fliction, an' I gwine will all my proputy to you.' Well, I don't want to tek de money, an' she des mos' nigh fo'ce it on me, so I say yes, an' Brothah Buford he des sot an' talk to us, an' he say dat he come to-morro' to bring a lawyer to draw up de will. But bless Gawd, honey, Sis' Callender died dat night, an' de will wasn't made, so when Brothah Buford come bright an' early next mornin', I was layin' Sis' Callender out. Brothah Buford was mighty much moved, he was. I nevah did see a strange pusson tek anything so hard in all my life, an' den he talk to me, an' he say, 'Now, Sis' Dicey, is you notified any de neighbours yit?' an' I said no I hain't notified no one of de neighbours, case I ain't 'quainted wid none o' dem yit, an' he say, 'How erbout de doctah? Is he 'quainted wid de diseased?' an' I tol' him no, he des come in, da's all. 'Well,' he say, 'cose you un'erstan' now dat you is Sis' Jane Callender, caise you inhe'it huh name, an' when de doctah come to mek out de 'stiffycate, you mus' tell him dat Sis' Dicey Fairfax is de name of de diseased, an' it 'll be all right, an' aftah dis you got to go by de name o' Jane Callender, caise it's a bus'ness name you done inhe'it.' Well, dat's whut I done, an' dat's huccome I been Jane Callender in de bus'ness 'sactions, an' Dicey Fairfax at home. Now, you un'erstan', don't you? It wuz my inhe'ited name."

"But don't you know that what you have done is a penitentiary offence?"

"Who you stan'in' up talkin' to dat erway, you nasty impident little scoun'el? Don't you talk to me dat erway. I reckon ef yo' mammy was hyeah she sut'ny would tend to yo' case. You alluse was sassier an' pearter den yo' brother Nelse, an' he had to go an' git killed in de wah, an' you—you—w'y, jedge, I'se spanked dat boy mo' times den I kin tell you fu' hus impidence. I don't see how you evah gits erlong wid him."

The court repressed a ripple that ran around. But there was no smile on the smooth-shaven, clear-cut face of the young Southerner. Turning to the attorney for the defence, he said: "Will you take the witness?" But that gentleman, waving one helpless hand, shook his head.

"That will do, then," said young Fairfax. "Your Honor," he went on, addressing the court, "I have no desire to prosecute this case further. You all see the trend of it just as I see, and it would be folly to continue the examination of any of the rest of these witnesses. We have got that story from Aunt Dicey herself as straight as an arrow from a bow. While technically she is guilty; while according to the facts she is a criminal according to the motive and the intent of her actions, she is as innocent as the whitest soul among us." He could not repress the youthful Southerner's love for this little bit of rhetoric.

"And I believe that nothing is to be gained by going further into the matter, save for the purpose of finding out the whereabouts of this Brother Buford, and attending to his case as the facts warrant. But before we do this, I want to see the stamp of crime wiped away from the name of my Aunt Dicey there, and I beg leave of the court to enter a *nolle prosse*. There is only one other thing I must ask of Aunt Dicey, and that is that she return the money that was illegally gotten, and give us information concerning the whereabouts of Buford."

Aunt Dicey looked up in excitement, "W'y, chile, ef dat money was got illegal, I don' want it, but I do know whut I gwine to do, cause I done 'vested it all wid Brothah Buford in his colorednization comp'ny." The court drew its breath. It had been expecting some such *dénouement*.

"And where is the office of this company situated?"

"Well, I des can't tell dat," said the old lady. "W'y, la, man, Brothah Buford was in co't to-day. Whaih is he? Brothah Buford, whaih you?" But no answer came from the surrounding spectators. Brother Buford had faded away. The old lady, however, after due conventions, was permitted to go home.

It was with joy in her heart that Aunt Dicey Fairfax went back to her little cottage after her dismissal, but her face clouded when soon after Robert Fairfax came in.

"Hyeah you come as usual," she said with well-feigned anger. "Tryin' to sof' soap me aftah you been carryin' on. You ain't changed one mite fu' all yo' bein' a man. What you talk to me dat away in co't fu'?"

Fairfax's face was very grave. "It was necessary, Aunt Dicey," he said. "You know I'm a lawyer now, and there are certain things that lawyers have to do whether they like it or not. You don't understand. That man Buford is a scoundrel, and he came very near leading you into a very dangerous and criminal act. I am glad I was near to save you."

"Oh, honey, chile, I didn't know dat. Set down an' tell me all erbout it."

This the attorney did, and the old lady's indignation blazed forth. "Well, I hope to de Lawd you'll fin' dat rascal an' larrup him ontwell he cain't stan' straight."

"No, we're going to do better than that and a great deal better. If we find him we are going to send him where he won't inveigle any more innocent people into rascality, and you're going to help us."

"W'y, sut'ny, chile, I'll do all I kin to he'p you git dat rascal, but I don't know whaih he lives, case he's allus come hyeah to see me."

"He'll come back some day. In the meantime we will be laying for him."

Aunt Dicey was putting some very flaky biscuits into the oven, and perhaps the memory of other days made the young lawyer prolong his visit and his explanation. When, however, he left, it was with well-laid plans to catch Jason Buford napping.

It did not take long. Stealthily that same evening a tapping came at Aunt Dicey's door. She opened it, and a small, crouching figure crept in. It was Mr. Buford. He turned down the collar of his coat which he had had closely up about his face and said:

"Well, well, Sis' Callender, you sut'ny have spoiled us all."

"La, Brothah Buford, come in hyeah an' set down. Whaih you been?"

"I been hidin' fu' feah of that testimony you give in the court room. What did you do that fu'?"

"La, me, I didn't know, you didn't 'splain to me in de fust."

"Well, you see, you spoiled it, an' I've got to git out of town as soon as I kin. Sis' Callender, dese hyeah white people is mighty slippery, and they might catch me. But I want to beg you to go on away from hyeah so's you won't be hyeah to testify if dey does. Hyeah's a hundred dollars of yo' money right down, and you leave hyeah to-morrer mornin' an' go erway as far as you kin git."

"La, man, I's puffectly willin' to he'p you, you know dat."

"Cose, cose," he answered hurriedly, "we col'red people has got to stan' together."

"But what about de res' of dat money dat I been 'vestin' wid you?"

"I'm goin' to pay intrus' on that," answered the promoter glibly.

"All right, all right." Aunt Dicey had made several trips to the little back room just off her sitting room as she talked with the promoter. Three times in the window had she waved a lighted lamp. Three times without success. But at the last "all right," she went into the room again. This time the waving lamp was answered by the sudden flash of a lantern outside.

"All right," she said, as she returned to the room, "set down an' lemme fix you some suppah."

"I ain't hardly got the time. I got to git away from hyeah." But the smell of the new baked biscuits was in his nostrils and he could not resist the temptation to sit down. He was eating hastily, but with appreciation, when the door opened and two minions of the law entered.

Buford sprang up and turned to flee, but at the back door, her large form a towering and impassive barrier, stood Aunt Dicey.

"Oh, don't hu'y, Brothah Buford," she said calmly, "set down an' he'p yo'se'f. Dese hyeah's my friends."

It was the next day that Robert Fairfax saw him in his cell. The man's face was ashen with coward's terror. He was like a caught rat though, bitingly on the defensive.

"You see we've got you, Buford," said Fairfax coldly to him. "It is as well to confess."

"I ain't got nothin' to say," said Buford cautiously.

"You will have something to say later on unless you say it now. I don't want to intimidate you, but Aunt Dicey's word will be taken in any court in the United States against yours, and I see a few years hard labour for you between good stout walls."

The little promoter showed his teeth in an impotent snarl. "What do you want me to do?" he asked, weakening.

"First, I want you to give back every cent of the money that you got out of Dicey Fairfax. Second, I want you to give up to every one of those Negroes that you have cheated every cent of the property you have accumulated by fraudulent means. Third, I want you to leave this place, and never come back so long as God leaves breath in your dirty body. If you do this, I will save you—you are not worth the saving—from the pen or worse. If you don't, I will make this place so hot for you that hell will seem like an ice-box beside it."

The little yellow man was cowering in his cell before the attorney's indignation. His lips were drawn back over his teeth in something that was neither a snarl nor a smile. His eyes were bulging and fear-stricken, and his hands clasped and unclasped themselves nervously.

"I—I——" he faltered, "do you want to send me out without a cent?"

"Without a cent, without a cent," said Fairfax tensely.

"I won't do it," the rat in him again showed fight. "I won't do it. I'll stay hyeah an' fight you. You can't prove anything on me."

"All right, all right," and the attorney turned toward the door.

"Wait, wait," called the man, "I will do it, my God! I will do it. Jest let me out o' hyeah, don't keep me caged up. I'll go away from hyeah."

Fairfax turned back to him coldly, "You will keep your word?"

"Yes."

"I will return at once and take the confession."

And so the thing was done. Jason Buford, stripped of his ill-gotten gains, left the neighbourhood of Little Africa forever. And Aunt Dicey, no longer a wealthy woman and a capitalist, is baking golden brown biscuits for a certain young attorney and his wife, who has the bad habit of rousing her anger by references to her business name and her investments with a promoter.

X

THE WISDOM OF SILENCE

JEREMIAH ANDERSON WAS FREE. He had been free for ten years, and he was proud of it. He had been proud of it from the beginning, and that was the reason that he was one of the first to cast off the bonds of his old relations, and move from the plantation and take up land for himself. He was anxious to cut himself off from all that bound him to his former life. So strong was this feeling in him that he would not consent to stay on and work for his one-time owner even for a full wage.

To the proposition of the planter and the gibes of some of his more dependent fellows he answered, "No, suh, I's free, an' I sholy is able to tek keer o' myse'f. I done been fattenin' frogs fu' othah people's snakes too long now."

"But, Jerry," said Samuel Brabant, "I don't mean you any harm. The thing's done. You don't belong to me any more, but naturally, I take an interest in you, and want to do what I can to give you a start. It's more than the Northern government has done for you, although such wise men ought to know that you have had no training in caring for yourselves."

There was a slight sneer in the Southerner's voice. Jerry perceived it and thought it directed against him. Instantly his pride rose and his neck stiffened.

"Nemmine me," he answered, "nemmine me. I's free, an' w'en a man's free, he's free."

"All right, go your own way. You may have to come back to me some time. If you have to come, come. I don't blame you now. It must be a great thing to you, this dream—this nightmare." Jerry looked at him. "Oh, it isn't a nightmare now, but some day, maybe, it will be, then come to me."

71

The master turned away from the newly made freeman, and Jerry went forth into the world which was henceforth to be his. He took with him his few belongings; these largely represented by his wife and four lusty-eating children. Besides, he owned a little money, which he had got working for others when his master's task was done. Thus, burdened and equipped, he set out to tempt Fortune.

He might do one of two things—farm land upon shares for one of his short-handed neighbours, or buy a farm, mortgage it, and pay for it as he could. As was natural for Jerry, and not uncommendable, he chose at once the latter course, bargained for his twenty acres—for land was cheap then, bought his mule, built his cabin, and set up his household goods.

Now, slavery may give a man the habit of work, but it cannot imbue him with the natural thrift that long years of self-dependence brings. There were times when Jerry's freedom tugged too strongly at his easy inclination, drawing him away to idle when he should have toiled. What was the use of freedom, asked an inward voice, if one might not rest when one would? If he might not stop midway the furrow to listen and laugh at a droll story or tell one? If he might not go a-fishing when all the forces of nature invited and the jay-bird called from the tree and gave forth saucy banter like the fiery, blue shrew that she was?

There were times when his compunction held Jerry to his task, but more often he turned an end furrow and laid his misgivings snugly under it and was away to the woods or the creek. There was joy and a loaf for the present. What more could he ask?

The first year Fortune laughed at him, and her laugh is very different from her smile. She sent the swift rains to wash up the new planted seed, and the hungry birds to devour them. She sent the fierce sun to scorch the young crops, and the clinging weeds to hug the fresh greenness of his hope to death. She sent—cruellest jest of all—another baby to be fed, and so weakened Cindy Ann that for many days she could not work beside her husband in the fields.

Poverty began to teach the unlessoned delver in the soil the thrift which he needed; but he ended his first twelve months with barely enough to eat, and nothing paid on his land or his mule. Broken and discouraged, the words of his old master came to him. But he was proud with an obstinate pride and he shut his lips together so that he might not groan. He would not go to his master. Anything rather than that.

In that place sat certain beasts of prey, dealers, and lenders of money, who had their lairs somewhere within the boundaries of that wide and mysterious domain called The Law. They had their risks to run, but so must all beasts that eat flesh or drink blood. To them went Jerry, and they were kind to him. They gave him of their store. They gave him food and seed, but they were to own all that they gave him from what he raised, and they were to take their toll first from the new crops.

Now, the black had been warned against these same beasts, for others had fallen a prey to them even in so short a time as their emancipation measured, and they saw themselves the re-manacled slaves of a hopeless and ever-growing debt, but Jerry would not be warned. He chewed the warnings like husks between his teeth, and got no substance from them.

Then, Fortune, who deals in surprises, played him another trick. She smiled upon him. His second year was better than his first, and the brokers swore over his paid up note. Cindy Ann was strong again and the oldest boy was big enough to help with the work.

Samuel Brabant was displeased, not because he felt any malice toward his former servant, but for the reason that any man with the natural amount of human vanity must feel himself agrieved just as his cherished prophecy is about to come true. Isaiah himself could not have been above it. How much less, then, the uninspired Mr. Brabant, who had his "I told you so," all ready. He had been ready to help Jerry after giving him admonitions, but here it was not needed. An unused "I told you so," however kindly, is an acid that turns the milk of human kindness sour.

Jerry went on gaining in prosperity. The third year treated him better than the second, and the fourth better than the third. During the fifth he enlarged his farm and his house and took pride in the fact that his oldest boy, Matthew, was away at school. By the tenth year of his freedom he was arrogantly out of debt. Then his pride was too much for him. During all these years of his struggle the words of his master had been as gall in his mouth. Now he spat them out with a boast. He talked much in the market-place, and where many people gathered, he was much there, giving himself as a bright and shining example.

"Huh," he would chuckle to any listeners he could find, "Ol' Mas' Brabant, he say, 'Stay hyeah, stay hyeah, you do' know how to tek keer o' yo'se'f yit.' But I des' look at my two han's an' I say to myse'f, whut I been doin' wid dese all dese yeahs—tekin' keer o' myse'f an' him, too. I wo'k in de fiel', he set in de big house an' smoke. I wo'k in de fiel', his son go away to college an' come back a graduate. Das hit. Well, w'en freedom come, I des' bent an' boun' I ain' gwine do it no mo' an' I didn't. Now look at me. I sets down w'en I wants to. I does my own wo'kin' an' my own smokin'. I don't owe a cent, an' dis yeah my boy gwine graduate f'om de school. Dat's me, an' I ain' called on ol' Mas' yit."

Now, an example is always an odious thing, because, first of all, it is always insolent even when it is bad, and there were those who listened to Jerry who had not been so successful as he, some even who had stayed on the plantation and as yet did not even own the mule they ploughed with. The hearts of those were filled with rage and their mouths with envy. Some of the sting of the latter got into their re-telling of Jerry's talk and made it worse than it was.

Old Samuel Brabant laughed and said, "Well, Jerry's not dead yet, and although I don't wish him any harm, my prophecy might come true yet."

There were others who, hearing, did not laugh, or if they did, it was with a mere strained thinning of the lips that had no element of mirth in it. Temper and tolerance were short ten years after sixty-three.

The foolish farmer's boastings bore fruit, and one night when he and his family had gone to church he returned to find his house and barn in ashes, his mules burned and his crop ruined. It had been very quietly done and quickly. The glare against the sky had attracted few from the nearby town, and them too late to be of service.

Jerry camped that night across the road from what remained of his former dwelling. Cindy Ann and the children, worn out and worried, went to sleep in spite of themselves, but he sat there all night long, his chin between his knees, gazing at what had been his pride.

Well, the beasts lay in wait for him again, and when he came to them they showed their fangs in greeting. And the velvet was over their claws. He had escaped them before. He had impugned their skill in the hunt, and they were ravenous for him. Now he was fatter, too. He went away from them with hard terms, and a sickness at his heart. But he had not said "Yes" to the terms. He was going home to consider the almost hopeless conditions under which they would let him build again.

They were staying with a neighbour in town pending his negotiations and thither he went to ponder on his circumstances. Then it was that Cindy Ann came into the equation. She demanded to know what was to be done and how it was to be gone about.

"But Cindy Ann, honey, you do' know nuffin' 'bout bus'ness."

"T'ain't whut I knows, but whut I got a right to know," was her response.

"I do' see huccome you got any right to be a-pryin' into dese hyeah things."

"I's got de same right I had to w'ok an' struggle erlong an' he'p you get whut we's done los'."

Jerry winced and ended by telling her all.

"Dat ain't nuffin' but owdacious robbery," said Cindy Ann. "Dem people sees dat you got a little some'p'n, an' dey ain't gwine stop ontwell dey's bu'nt an' stoled evah blessed cent f'om you. Je'miah, don't you have nuffin' mo' to do wid 'em."

"I got to, Cindy Ann."

"Whut fu' you got to?"

"How I gwine buil' a cabin an' a ba'n an' buy a mule less'n I deal wid 'em?"

"Dah's Mas' Sam Brabant. He'd he'p you out."

Jerry rose up, his eyes flashing fire. "Cindy Ann," he said, "you a fool, you ain't got no mo' pride den a guinea hen, an' you got a heap less sense. W'y, befo' I go to ol' Mas' Sam Brabant fu' a cent, I'd sta've out in de road."

"Huh!" said Cindy Ann, shutting her mouth on her impatience.

One gets tired of thinking and saying how much more sense a woman has than a man when she comes in where his sense stops and his pride begins.

With the recklessness of despair Jerry slept late that next morning, but he might have awakened early without spoiling his wife's plans. She was up betimes, had gone on her mission and returned before her spouse awoke.

It was about ten o'clock when Brabant came to see him. Jerry grew sullen at once as his master approached, but his pride stiffened. This white man should see that misfortune could not weaken him.

"Well, Jerry," said his former master, "you would not come to me, eh, so I must come to you. You let a little remark of mine keep you from your best friend, and put you in the way of losing the labour of years."

Jerry made no answer.

"You've proved yourself able to work well, but Jerry," pausing, "you haven't yet shown that you're able to take care of yourself, you don't know how to keep your mouth shut."

The ex-slave tried to prove this a lie by negative pantomime.

"I'm going to lend you the money to start again."

"I won't——"

"Yes, you will, if you don't, I'll lend it to Cindy Ann, and let her build in her own name. She's got more sense than you, and she knows how to keep still when things go well."

"Mas' Sam," cried Jerry, rising quickly, "don' len' dat money to Cindy Ann. W'y ef a ooman's got anything she nevah lets you hyeah de las' of it."

"Will you take it, then?"

"Yes, suh; yes, suh, an' thank 'e, Mas' Sam." There were sobs some place back in his throat. "An' nex' time ef I evah gets a sta't agin, I'll keep my mouf shet. Fac' is, I'll come to you, Mas' Sam, an' borry fu' de sake o' hidin'."

XI

THE TRIUMPH OF OL' MIS' PEASE

BETWEEN THE TWO WOMEN, the feud began in this way: When Ann
Pease divorced her handsome but profligate spouse, William,
Nancy Rogers had, with reprehensible haste, taken him for better
or for worse. Of course, it proved for worse, but Ann Pease had
never forgiven her.

"'Pears lak to me," she said, "dat she was des a-waitin' fu' to step
inter my shoes, no mattah how I got outen 'em, whethah I died or
divo'ced."

It was in the hey-day of Nancy Rogers' youth, and she was still
hot-tempered, so she retorted that "Ann Pease sut'ny did unmind
huh' o' de dawg in de mangah." The friends of the two women
took sides, and a war began which waged hotly between them—a
war which for the first few weeks threatened the unity of Mt.
Pisgah Church.

But the church in all times has been something of a selfish insti-
tution and has known how to take care of itself. Now, Mt. Pisgah,
of necessity, must recognise divorce, and of equal necessity, re-
marriage. So when the Rev. Isaiah Johnson had been appealed to,
he had spread his fat hands, closed his eyes and said solemnly,
"Whom God hath j'ined, let no man put asundah;" peace, or at
best, apparent peace, settled upon the troubled waters.

The solidity of Mt. Pisgah was assured, the two factions again
spoke to each other, both gave collections on the same Sunday; but
between the two principals there was no abatement of their relentless animosity.

Ann Pease as it happened was a "puffessor," while the new Mrs.
Pease was out of the fold; a gay, frivolous person who had never
sought or found grace. She laughed when a black wag said of the

two that "they might bofe be 'peas,' but dey wasn't out o' de same pod." But on its being repeated to Sister Pease, she resented it with Christian indignation, sniffed and remarked that "Ef Wi'yum choosed to pick out one o' de onregenerate an' hang huh ez a mill-stone erroun' his neck, it wasn't none o' huh bus'ness what happened to him w'en dey pulled up de tares f'om de wheat."

There were some ultra-malicious ones who said that Sister Pease, seeing her former husband in the possession of another, had begun to regret her step, for the unregenerate William was good-looking after all, and the "times" that he and his equally sinful wife had together were the wonder and disgust, the envy and horror of the whole community, who watched them with varying moods of eagerness.

Sister Ann Pease went her way apparently undisturbed. Religion has an arrogance of its own, and when at the end of the year the good widow remained unmarried she could toss her head, go her way, and look down from a far height upon the "po' sinnahs"; indeed, she had rather the better of her frailer sister in the sympathies of the people.

As one sister feelingly remarked, "Dat ooman des baihin' dat man in huh prayahs, an' I 'low she'll mou'n him into glory yit."

One year of married life disillusions, and defiant gaiety cannot live upon itself when admiration fails. There is no reward in being daring when courage becomes commonplace. The year darkened to winter, and bloomed to spring again. The willows feathered along the river banks, and the horse-chestnuts budded and burst into beautiful life. Then came summer, rejoicing, with arms full of flowers, and autumn with lap full of apples and grain, then winter again, and all through the days Nancy danced and was gay, but there was a wistfulness in her eyes, and the tug of the baby no longer drew her heart. She had come to be "Wi'yum's Nancy," while the other *that* other was still "Sister Pease," who sat above her in the high places of the people's hearts.

And then, oh, blessedness of the winter, the revival came; and both she and William, strangely stricken together with the realisation of their sins, fell at the mercy seat.

"There is more joy over one sinner that repenteth,"—but when Will and Nancy both "came through" on the same night—well, Mt. Pisgah's walls know the story.

There was triumph in Nancy's face as she proclaimed her conversion, and the first person she made for was Sister Pease. She shook her hands and embraced her, crying ever aloud between the vociferations of the congregation, "Oh, sistah, he'p me praise Him, he'p me praise Him," and the elder woman in the cause caught the infection of the moment and joined in the general shout.

Afterwards she was not pleased with herself. But then if she hadn't shouted, wouldn't it have been worse?

The Rev. Isaiah was nothing if not dramatic in his tendencies, and on the day when he was to receive William and Nancy Pease into full membership with the church, it struck him that nothing could make upon his congregation a profounder impression for good than to have the two new Peases joined by the elder one, or as the wag would have put it, all in one pod. And it was so ordered, and the thing was done.

It is true that the preacher had to labour some with Sister Ann Pease, but when he showed her how it was her Christian duty, and if she failed of it her rival must advance before her in public opinion, she acquiesced. It was an easier matter with "Sister Wi'yum Pease." She agreed readily, for she was filled with condescending humility, which on every occasion she took the opportunity of displaying toward her rival.

The Rev. Isaiah Johnson only made one mistake in his diplomatic manoeuvring. That was when he whispered to Sister Ann Pease, "Didn't I tell you? Des see how easy Sister Wi'yum give in." He was near to losing his cause and the wind was completely taken out of his sails when the widow replied with a snort, "Give in, my Lawd! Dat ooman's got a right to give in; ain't she got 'uligion an' de man, too?"

However, the storm blew over, and by the time service was begun they were all seated together on a front bench, Sister Nancy, William, and Sister Ann.

Now was the psychological moment, and after a soul-stirring hymn the preacher rose and announced his text—"Behold how good and how pleasant it is for brethren to dwell together in unity."

Someone in the back part of the church suggested trinity as a substitute and started a titter, but the preacher had already got his dramatic momentum, and was sweeping along in a tumultuous tide of oratory. Right at his three victims did he aim his fiery eloquence, and ever and again he came back to his theme, "Behold how good and how pleasant it is for brethren to dwell together in unity," even though Ann Pease had turned her back on William, whose head was low bowed, and Nancy was ostentatiously weeping into a yellow silk handkerchief.

The sermon spurred on to a tempestuous close, and then came the climax when the doors of the church were opened. William and Nancy immediately went up to end their probation, and after a few whispered remarks the minister shook hands with each of them, then raising his voice he said: "Now, brothahs and sistahs, befo' you all gives dese lambs de right han' o' fellowship to welcome dem to de fol', I want Sister Ann Pease to come up an' be de first to bid 'em God speed on the gospel way." Ann Pease visibly swelled, but she marched up, and without looking at either, shook hands with each of her enemies.

"Hallelujah, praise de Lord," shouted the preacher, clapping his hands, "Behold how good and how pleasant it is; and now let the congregation in gineral come aroun' and welcome Brothah and Sistah Pease."

His rich bass voice broke into "Bless Be the Tie that Binds," and as the volume of the hymn, swelled by the full chorus of the congregation, rolled away to the rafters of the little church, the people rose and marched solemnly round, shaking hands with the new members and with each other.

Brother and Sister Pease were the last to leave church that day, but they found Ann waiting for them at door. She walked straight up to them and spoke: "Nancy Rogers," she said, "I know you; I kin see claih thoo you, and you ain't a foolin' me one bit. All I got to say is dat I has done my Christian duty, an' I ain't gwine do no mo', so don' you speak to me fo'm dis day out."

For the brief space of a second there was something like a gleam in Nancy's eyes, but she replied in all meekness, "I's a full-blown Christian now, an' I feel it my bounden duty to speak to you, Sis' Pease, an' I's gwine t' speak."

Ignoring this defiance the other woman turned to her former husband. She looked at him with unveiled contempt, then she said slowly, "An' ez fu' Wi'yum, Gawd he'p you."

Here all intercourse between these warring spirits might have ended but for Nancy Pease's persistent civility. She would speak to her rival on every occasion, and even call upon her if she could gain admittance to the house. And now the last drop of bitterness fell into the widow's cup, for the community, to distinguish between them, began calling her "Ol' Sis' Pease." This was the climax of her sorrows, and she who had been so devout came no more to the church; she who had been so cheerful and companionable grew morose and sour and shut her doors against her friends. She was as one dead to her old world. The one bit of vivid life about her was her lasting hatred of the woman who bore her name. In vain the preacher sought to break down the barrier of her animosity. She had built it of adamant, and his was a losing fight. So for several years the feud went on, and those who had known Ann in her cheerier days forgot that knowledge and spoke of her with open aversion as "dat awful ol' Mis' Pease." The while Nancy, in spite of "Wi'yum's" industrial vagaries, had flourished and waxed opulent. She continued to flaunt her Christian humility in the eyes of her own circle, and to withhold her pity from the poor, lonely old woman whom hate had made bitter and to whom the world, after all, had not been over-kind. But prosperity is usually cruel, and one needs the prick of the thorn one's self to know how it stings his brother.

She was startled one day, however, out of her usual placidity. Sister Martin, one of her neighbours, dropped in and settling herself with a sigh announced the important news, "Well, bless Gawd, ol' Sis' Pease is gone at last."

Nancy dropped the plate she had been polishing, and unheeded, it smashed into bits on the floor.

"Wha'—what!" she exclaimed.

"Yes'm," Sister Martin assured her, "de ol' lady done passed away."

"I didn't know she was sick; w'en she die?"

"She done shet huh eyes on dis worl' o' sorror des a few minutes ago. She ain't bin sick mo'n two days."

Nancy had come to herself now, and casting her eyes up in an excess of Christian zeal, she said: "Well, she wouldn't let me do nuffin' fu' huh in life, but I sut'ny shell try to do my duty by huh in death," and drying her hands and throwing a shawl over her head, she hastened over to her dead enemy's house.

The news had spread quickly and the neighbourhood had just begun to gather in the little room which held the rigid form. Nancy entered and made her way through the group about the bed, waving the others aside imperiously.

"It is my Christian duty," she said solemnly, "to lay Sis' Pease out, an' I's gwine do it." She bent over the bed. Now there are a dozen truthful women who will vouch for the truth of what happened. When Nancy leaned over the bed, as if in obedience to the power of an electric shock, the corpse's eyes flew open, Ann Pease rose up in bed and pointing a trembling finger at her frightened namesake exclaimed: "Go 'way f'om me, Nancy Rogers, don't you daih to tech me. You ain't got de come-uppance of me yit. Don't you daih to lay me out."

Most of this remark, it seems, fell on empty air, for the room was cleared in a twinkling. Women holding high numerous skirts over their heavy shoes fled in a panic, and close in their wake panted Nancy Pease.

There have been conflicting stories about the matter, but there are those who maintain that after having delivered her ultimatum, old Mis' Pease immediately resumed the natural condition of a dead person. In fact there was no one there to see, and the old lady did not really die until night, and when they found her, there was a smile of triumph on her face.

Nancy did not help to lay her out.

XII

THE LYNCHING OF JUBE BENSON

GORDON FAIRFAX'S LIBRARY held but three men, but the air was dense with clouds of smoke. The talk had drifted from one topic to another much as the smoke wreaths had puffed, floated, and thinned away. Then Handon Gay, who was an ambitious young reporter, spoke of a lynching story in a recent magazine, and the matter of punishment without trial put new life into the conversation.

"I should like to see a real lynching," said Gay rather callously.

"Well, I should hardly express it that way," said Fairfax, "but if a real, live lynching were to come my way, I should not avoid it."

"I should," spoke the other from the depths of his chair, where he had been puffing in moody silence. Judged by his hair, which was freely sprinkled with gray, the speaker might have been a man of forty-five or fifty, but his face, though lined and serious, was youthful, the face of a man hardly past thirty.

"What, you, Dr. Melville? Why, I thought that you physicians wouldn't weaken at anything."

"I have seen one such affair," said the doctor gravely, "in fact, I took a prominent part in it."

"Tell us about it," said the reporter, feeling for his pencil and note-book, which he was, nevertheless, careful to hide from the speaker.

The men drew their chairs eagerly up to the doctor's, but for a minute he did not seem to see them, but sat gazing abstractedly into the fire, then he took a long draw upon his cigar and began:

"I can see it all very vividly now. It was in the summer time and about seven years ago. I was practising at the time down in the little town of Bradford. It was a small and primitive place, just the location for an impecunious medical man, recently out of college.

83

"In lieu of a regular office, I attended to business in the first of two rooms which I rented from Hiram Daly, one of the more prosperous of the townsmen. Here I boarded and here also came my patients—white and black—whites from every section, and blacks from 'nigger town,' as the west portion of the place was called.

"The people about me were most of them coarse and rough, but they were simple and generous, and as time passed on I had about abandoned my intention of seeking distinction in wider fields and determined to settle into the place of a modest country doctor. This was rather a strange conclusion for a young man to arrive at, and I will not deny that the presence in the house of my host's beautiful young daughter, Annie, had something to do with my decision. She was a beautiful young girl of seventeen or eighteen, and very far superior to her surroundings. She had a native grace and a pleasing way about her that made everybody that came under her spell her abject slave. White and black who knew her loved her, and none, I thought, more deeply and respectfully than Jube Benson, the black man of all work about the place.

"He was a fellow whom everybody trusted; an apparently steady-going, grinning sort, as we used to call him. Well, he was completely under Miss Annie's thumb, and would fetch and carry for her like a faithful dog. As soon as he saw that I began to care for Annie, and anybody could see that, he transferred some of his allegiance to me and became my faithful servitor also. Never did a man have a more devoted adherent in his wooing than did I, and many a one of Annie's tasks which he volunteered to do gave her an extra hour with me. You can imagine that I liked the boy and you need not wonder any more that as both wooing and my practice waxed apace, I was content to give up my great ambitions and stay just where I was.

"It wasn't a very pleasant thing, then, to have an epidemic of typhoid break out in the town that kept me going so that I hardly had time for the courting that a fellow wants to carry on with his sweetheart while he is still young enough to call her his girl. I fumed, but duty was duty, and I kept to my work night and day. It was now that Jube proved how invaluable he was as a coadjutor. He not only took messages to Annie, but brought sometimes little ones from her to me, and he would tell me little secret things that he had overheard her say that made me throb with joy and swear at him for repeating his mistress' conversation. But best of all, Jube was a perfect Cerberus, and no one on earth could have been more effective in keeping away or deluding the other young fellows who visited the Dalys. He would tell me of it afterwards, chuckling softly to himself. "'An', Doctah,' I say to Mistah Hemp Stevens, "'Scuse us, Mistah Stevens, but Miss Annie, she des gone out,' an' den he go outer de gate lookin' moughty lonesome. When Sam Elkins come, I say, "Sh, Mistah Elkins, Miss Annie, she done tuk down," an' he say, "What, Jube, you don' reckon hit de——" Den he stop an' look skeert, an' I say, "I feared hit is, Mistah Elkins," an' sheks my haid ez solemn. He goes outer de gate lookin' lak his bes' frien' done daid, an' all de time Miss Annie behine de cu'tain ovah de po'ch des' a laffin' fit to kill.'

"Jube was a most admirable liar, but what could I do? He knew that I was a young fool of a hypocrite, and when I would rebuke him for these deceptions, he would give way and roll on the floor in an excess of delighted laughter until from very contagion I had to join him—and, well, there was no need of my preaching when there had been no beginning to his repentance and when there must ensue a continuance of his wrong-doing.

"This thing went on for over three months, and then, pouf! I was down like a shot. My patients were nearly all up, but the reaction from overwork made me an easy victim of the lurking germs. Then Jube loomed up as a nurse. He put everyone else aside, and with the doctor, a friend of mine from a neighbouring town, took entire charge of me. Even Annie herself was put aside, and I was cared for as tenderly as a baby. Tom, that was my physician and friend, told me all about it afterward with tears in his eyes. Only he was a big, blunt man and his expressions did not convey all that he meant. He told me how my nigger had nursed me as if I were a sick kitten and he my mother. Of how fiercely he guarded his right to be the sole one to 'do' for me, as he called it, and how, when the crisis came, he hovered, weeping, but hopeful, at my bedside, until it was safely passed, when they drove him, weak and exhausted, from the room. As for me, I knew little about it at the time, and cared less. I was too busy in my fight with death. To my chimerical vision there was only a black but gentle demon that came and went, alternating with a white fairy, who would insist on coming in on her head, growing larger and larger and then dissolving. But the pathos and devotion in the story lost nothing in my blunt friend's telling.

"It was during the period of a long convalescence, however, that I came to know my humble ally as he really was, devoted to the point of abjectness. There were times when for very shame at his goodness to me, I would beg him to go away, to do something else. He would go, but before I had time to realise that I was not being ministered to, he would be back at my side, grinning and pottering just the same. He manufactured duties for the joy of performing them. He pretended to see desires in me that I never had, because he liked to pander to them, and when I became entirely exasperated, and ripped out a good round oath, he chuckled with the remark, 'Dah, now, you sholy is gittin' well. Nevah did hyeah a man anywhaih nigh Jo'dan's sho' cuss lak dat.'

"Why, I grew to love him, love him, oh, yes, I loved him as well—oh, what am I saying? All human love and gratitude are damned poor things; excuse me, gentlemen, this isn't a pleasant story. The truth is usually a nasty thing to stand.

"It was not six months after that that my friendship to Jube, which he had been at such great pains to win, was put to too severe a test.

"It was in the summer time again, and as business was slack, I had ridden over to see my friend, Dr. Tom. I had spent a good part of the day there, and it was past four o'clock when I rode leisurely into Bradford. I was in a particularly joyous mood and no premonition of the impending catastrophe oppressed me. No sense of sorrow, present or to come, forced itself upon me, even when I saw men hurrying through the almost deserted streets. When I got within sight of my home and saw a crowd surrounding it, I was only interested sufficiently to spur my horse into a jog trot, which brought me up to the throng, when something in the sullen, settled horror in the men's faces gave me a sudden, sick thrill. They whispered a word to me, and without a thought, save for Annie, the girl who had been so surely growing into my heart, I leaped from the saddle and tore my way through the people to the house.

"It was Annie, poor girl, bruised and bleeding, her face and dress torn from struggling. They were gathered round her with white faces, and, oh, with what terrible patience they were trying to gain from her fluttering lips the name of her murderer. They made way for me and I knelt at her side. She was beyond my skill, and my will merged with theirs. One thought was in our minds.

"'Who?' I asked.

"Her eyes half opened, 'That black——' She fell back into my arms dead.

"We turned and looked at each other. The mother had broken down and was weeping, but the face of the father was like iron.

"'It is enough,' he said; 'Jube has disappeared.' He went to the door and said to the expectant crowd, 'She is dead.'

"I heard the angry roar without swelling up like the noise of a flood, and then I heard the sudden movement of many feet as the men separated into searching parties, and laying the dead girl back upon her couch, I took my rifle and went out to join them.

"As if by intuition the knowledge had passed among the men that Jube Benson had disappeared, and he, by common consent, was to be the object of our search. Fully a dozen of the citizens had seen him hastening toward the woods and noted his skulking air, but as he had grinned in his old good-natured way they had, at the time, thought nothing of it. Now, however, the diabolical reason of his slyness was apparent. He had been shrewd enough to disarm suspicion, and by now was far away. Even Mrs. Daly, who was visiting with a neighbour, had seen him stepping out by a back way, and had said with a laugh, 'I reckon that black rascal's a-running off somewhere.' Oh, if she had only known.

"'To the woods! To the woods!' that was the cry, and away we went, each with the determination not to shoot, but to bring the culprit alive into town, and then to deal with him as his crime deserved.

"I cannot describe the feelings I experienced as I went out that night to beat the woods for this human tiger. My heart smouldered within me like a coal, and I went forward under the impulse of a will that was half my own, half some more malignant power's. My throat throbbed drily, but water nor whiskey would not have quenched my thirst. The thought has come to me since that now I could interpret the panther's desire for blood and sympathise with it, but then I thought nothing. I simply went forward, and watched, watched with burning eyes for a familiar form that I had looked for as often before with such different emotions.

"Luck or ill-luck, which you will, was with our party, and just as dawn was graying the sky, we came upon our quarry crouched in the corner of a fence. It was only half light, and we might have passed, but my eyes had caught sight of him, and I raised the cry. We levelled our guns and he rose and came toward us.

"'I t'ought you wa'n't gwine see me,' he said sullenly, 'I didn't mean no harm.'

"'Harm!'

"Some of the men took the word up with oaths, others were ominously silent.

"We gathered around him like hungry beasts, and I began to see terror dawning in his eyes. He turned to me, 'I's moughty glad you's hyeah, doc,' he said, 'you ain't gwine let 'em whup me.'

"'Whip you, you hound,' I said, 'I'm going to see you hanged,' and in the excess of my passion I struck him full on the mouth. He made a motion as if to resent the blow against even such great odds, but controlled himself.

"'W'y, doctah,' he exclaimed in the saddest voice I have ever heard, 'w'y, doctah! I ain't stole nuffin' o' yo'n, an' I was comin' back. I only run off to see my gal, Lucy, ovah to de Centah.'

"'You lie!' I said, and my hands were busy helping the others bind him upon a horse. Why did I do it? I don't know. A false education, I reckon, one false from the beginning. I saw his black face glooming there in the half light, and I could only think of him as a monster. It's tradition. At first I was told that the black man would catch me, and when I got over that, they taught me that the devil was black, and when I had recovered from the sickness of that belief, here were Jube and his fellows with faces of menacing blackness. There was only one conclusion: This black man stood for all the powers of evil, the result of whose machinations had been gathering in my mind from childhood up. But this has nothing to do with what happened.

"After firing a few shots to announce our capture, we rode back into town with Jube. The ingathering parties from all directions met us as we made our way up to the house. All was very quiet and orderly. There was no doubt that it was as the papers would have said, a gathering of the best citizens. It was a gathering of stern, determined men, bent on a terrible vengeance.

"We took Jube into the house, into the room where the corpse lay. At sight of it, he gave a scream like an animal's and his face went the colour of storm-blown water. This was enough to condemn him. We divined, rather than heard, his cry of 'Miss Ann, Miss Ann, oh, my God, doc, you don't t'ink I done it?'

"Hungry hands were ready. We hurried him out into the yard. A rope was ready. A tree was at hand. Well, that part was the least of it, save that Hiram Daly stepped aside to let me be the first to pull upon the rope. It was lax at first. Then it tightened, and I felt the quivering soft weight resist my muscles. Other hands joined, and Jube swung off his feet.

"No one was masked. We knew each other. Not even the culprit's face was covered, and the last I remember of him as he went into the air was a look of sad reproach that will remain with me until I meet him face to face again.

"We were tying the end of the rope to a tree, where the dead man might hang as a warning to his fellows, when a terrible cry chilled us to the marrow.

"'Cut 'im down, cut 'im down, he ain't guilty. We got de one. Cut him down, fu' Gawd's sake. Here's de man, we foun' him hidin' in de barn!'

"Jube's brother, Ben, and another Negro, came rushing toward us, half dragging, half carrying a miserable-looking wretch between them. Someone cut the rope and Jube dropped lifeless to the ground.

"'Oh, my Gawd, he's daid, he's daid!' wailed the brother, but with blazing eyes he brought his captive into the centre of the group, and we saw in the full light the scratched face of Tom Skinner—the worst white ruffian in the town—but the face we saw was not as we were accustomed to see it, merely smeared with dirt. It was blackened to imitate a Negro's.

"God forgive me; I could not wait to try to resuscitate Jube. I knew he was already past help, so I rushed into the house and to the dead girl's side. In the excitement they had not yet washed or laid her out. Carefully, carefully, I searched underneath her broken finger nails. There was skin there. I took it out, the little curled pieces, and went with it to my office.

"There, determinedly, I examined it under a powerful glass, and read my own doom. It was the skin of a white man, and in it were embedded strands of short, brown hair or beard.

"How I went out to tell the waiting crowd I do not know, for something kept crying in my ears, 'Blood guilty! Blood guilty!'

"The men went away stricken into silence and awe. The new prisoner attempted neither denial nor plea. When they were gone I would have helped Ben carry his brother in, but he waved me away fiercely, 'You he'ped murder my brothah, you dat was *his* frien', go 'way, go 'way! I'll tek him home myse'f.' I could only respect his wish, and he and his comrade took up the dead man and between them bore him up the street on which the sun was now shining full.

"I saw the few men who had not skulked indoors uncover as they passed, and I—I—stood there between the two murdered ones, while all the while something in my ears kept crying, 'Blood guilty! Blood guilty!'"

The doctor's head dropped into his hands and he sat for some time in silence, which was broken by neither of the men, then he rose, saying, "Gentlemen, that was my last lynching."

XIII

SCHWALLIGER'S PHILANTHROPY

THERE IS NO ADEQUATE REASON why Schwalliger's name should appear upon the pages of history. He was decidedly not in good society. He was not even respectable as respectability goes. But certain men liked him and certain women loved him. He is dead. That is all that will be said of the most of us after a while. He was but a weak member of the community, but those who loved him did not condemn him, and they shut their eyes to his shortcomings because they were a part of him. Without his follies he would not have been himself.

Schwalliger was only a race-horse "tout." Ah, don't hold up your hands, good friends, for circumstances of birth make most of us what we are, whether poets or pickpockets, and if this thick-set, bow-legged black man became a "tout" it was because he had to. Old horsemen will tell you that Schwalliger—no one knew where he got the name—was rolling and tumbling about the track at Bennings when he was still so short in stature that he got the name of the "tadpole." Naturally, he came to know much of horses, grew up with them, in fact, and having no wealthy father or mother to indulge him in his taste or help him use his knowledge, he did the next best thing and used his special education for himself in the humble capacity of voluntary adviser to aspiring gamesters. He prospered and blossomed out into good clothes of a highly ornate pattern. Naturally, like a man in any other business, he had his ups and downs, and there were times when the good clothes disappeared and he was temporarily forced to return to the occupation of rubbing down horses; but these periods of depression were of short duration, and at the next turn of fortune's wheel he would again be on top.

"No, thuh," he was wont to say, with his inimitable lisp—"no, thuh, you can't keep a good man down. 'Tain't no use a-talkin', you jeth can't. It don't do me no harm to go back to rubbin' now an' then. It jeth nachully keepth me on good termth with de hothes."

And, indeed, it did seem that his prophecies were surer and his knowledge more direct after one of these periods of enforced humility.

There were various things whispered about Schwalliger; that he was no more honest than he should be, that he was not as sound as he might be; but though it might be claimed, and was, that he would prophesy, on occasion, the success of three different horses to three different men, no one ever accused him of being less than fair with the women who came out from the city to enjoy the races and increase their excitement by staking small sums. To these Schwalliger was the soul of courtesy and honour, and if they lost upon his advice, he was not happy until he had made it up to them again.

One, however, who sets himself to work to give a racehorse tout a character may expect to have his labour for his pains. The profession of his subject is against him. He may as well put aside his energy and say, "Well, perhaps he was a bad lot, but——." The present story is not destined to put you more in love with the hero of it, but——

The heat and enthusiasm at Saratoga and the other race-courses was done, and autumn and the glory of Bennings had come. The ingratiating Schwalliger came back with the horses to his old stamping ground and to happiness. The other tracks had not treated him kindly, and but for the kindness of his equine friends, whom he slept with and tended, he might have come back to Washington on the wooden steps. But he was back, and that was happiness for him. Broke?

"Well," said Schwalliger, in answer to a trainer's question, "I ain't exactly broke, Misthah Johnthon, but I wath pretty badly bent. I goth awa jutht ath thoon ath I commenth to feel mythelf crackin', but I'm hyeah to git even."

He was only a rubber again, but he began to get even early in the week, and by Saturday he was again as like to a rainbow as any of his class. He did not, however, throw away his rubber's clothes. He was used to the caprices of fortune, and he did not know how soon again he should need them. That he was not dressed in them, and yet saved them, made him capable of performing his one philanthropy.

Had he not been gorgeously dressed he would not have inspired the confidence of the old Negro who came up to him on Tuesday morning, disconsolate and weeping.

"Mistah," he said deferentially through his tears, "is you a spo't?"

Mr. Schwalliger's chest protruded, and his very red lips opened in a smile as he answered: "Well, I do' know'th I'm tho much of a thpo't, but I think I knowth a thing or two."

"You look lak a spo'tin' gent'man, an' ef you is I thought mebbe you'd he'p me out."

"Wha'th the mattah? Up againtht it? You look a little ol' to be doin' the gay an' frithky." But Schwalliger's eyes were kind.

"Well, I'll tell you des' how it is, suh. I come f'om down in Ma'lan', 'case I wanted to see de hosses run. My ol' mastah was moughty fon' of sich spo't, an' I kin' o' likes it myse'f, dough I don't nevah bet, suh. I's a chu'ch membah. But yistiddy aftahnoon dee was two gent'men what I seen playin' wid a leetle ball an' some cups ovah it, an' I went up to look on, an' lo an' behol', suh, it was one o' dese money-mekin' t'ings. W'y, I seen de man des' stan' dere an' mek money by de fis'ful. Well, I 'low I got sorter wo'ked up. De men dee axed me to bet, but I 'low how I was a chu'ch membah an' didn't tek pa't in no sich carryin's on, an' den dee said 'twan't nuffin mo' den des' a chu'ch raffle, an' it was mo' fun den anyt'ing else. I des' say dat I could fin' de little ball, an' dee said I couldn't, an' if I fin' it dee gin me twenty dollahs, an' if I didn' I des' gin 'em ten dollahs. I shuk my haid. I wa'n't gwine be tempted, an' I try to pull myse'f erway. Ef I'd 'a' gone den 'twould 'a' been all right, but I stayed an' I stayed, an' I looked, an' I looked, an' it did seem lak it was so easy. At las', mistah, I tried it, an' I didn' fin' dat ball, an' dee got my ten dollahs, an' dat was all I had."

"Uh, huh," said Schwalliger grimly, "thell game, an' dey did you." The old man shuffled uneasily, but continued:

"Yes, suh, dee done me, an' de worst of it is, I's 'fraid to go home, even ef I could get dere, 'case dee boun' to axe me how I los' dat money, an' dee ain't no way fu' me to hide it, an' ef dee fin' out I been gamblin' I'll git chu'ched fu' it, an' I been a puffessor so long——" The old man's voice broke, and Schwalliger smiled the crooked smile of a man whose heart is touched.

"Whereth thith push wo'kin'?" he said briefly.

"Right ovah thaih," said the old Negro, indicating a part of the grounds not far distant.

"All right, you go on ovah thaih an' wait fu' me; an' if you thee me, remembah, you don't thee me. I don't know you, you don't know me, but I'll try to thee you out all right."

The old man went on his way, a new light in his eyes at the hope Schwalliger had inspired. Schwalliger himself made his way back to the stables; his dirty, horsy, rubber's outfit was there. He smiled intelligently as he looked at it. He was smiling in a different manner when, all dressed in it, he came up nearer to the grand stand. It was a very inane smile. He looked the very image of simplicity and ignorance, like a man who was anxious and ready to be duped. He strolled carelessly up to where the little game with the little ball was going on, and stood there looking foolishly on. The three young men—ostensibly there was only one—were doing a rushing business. They were playing very successfully on that trait of human nature which feels itself glorified and exalted when it has got something for nothing. The rustics, black and white, and some who had not the excuse of rusticity, were falling readily into the trap and losing their hard-earned money. Every now and then a man—one of their confederates, of course, would make a striking winning, and this served as a bait for the rest of the spectators. Schwalliger looked on with growing interest, always smiling an ignorant, simple smile. Finally, as if he could stand it no longer, he ran his hand in his pocket and pulled out a roll of money—money in its most beautiful and tempting form, the long, green notes. Then, as if a sudden spirit of prudence had taken possession of him, he put it back into his pocket, shook his head, and began working his way out of the crowd. But the operator of the shell game had caught sight of the bills, and it was like the scent of blood to the tiger. His eye was on the simple Negro at once, and he called cheerfully:

"Come up, uncle, and try your luck. See how I manipulate this ball. Easy enough to find if you're only lucky." He was so flippantly shrewd that his newness to the business was insolently apparent to Schwalliger, who knew a thing or two himself. Schwalliger smiled again and shook his head.

"Oh, no, thuh," he said, "I don't play dat."

"Why, come and try your luck anyhow; no harm in it."

Schwalliger took out his money and looked at it again and shook his head. He began again his backward movement from the crowd.

"No," he said, "I wouldn' play erroun' hyeah befo' all thethe people, becauthe you wouldn't pay me even ef I won."

"Why, of course we would," said the flippant operator; "every-body looks alike to us here."

Schwalliger kept moving away, ever and anon sending wistful, inane glances back at his tempter.

The bait worked admirably. The man closed up his little folding table, and, winking to his confederates, followed the retreating Negro. They stayed about with the crowd, while he followed on and on until Schwalliger had led him into a short alley between the stables. There he paused and allowed his pursuer to catch up with him.

"Thay, mithtah," he said, "what you keep on follerin' me fu'? I do' want to play wid you; I ain't got but fo'ty dollahs, an' ef I lothe I'll have to walk home."

"Why, my dear fellow, there ain't no way for you to lose. Come, now, let me show you." And he set the table down and began to manipulate the ball dexterously. "Needn't put no money down. Just see if you can locate the ball a few times for fun."

Schwalliger consented, and, greatly to his delight, located the little ball four times out of five. He was grinning now and the eye of the tempter was gleaming. Schwalliger took out his money.

"How much you got?" he said.

"Just eighty-five dollars, and I will lay it all against your forty."

"What you got it in?" asked Schwalliger.

"Four fives, four tens, and five five-dollar gold-pieces." And the man displayed it ostentatiously. The tout's eyes flashed as he saw his opponent put his money back into his waistcoat pocket.

"Well, I bet you," he said, and planked his money down.

The operator took the shells and swept the pea first under one then under the other, and laid the three side by side. Schwalliger laid his hand upon one. He lifted it up and there was nothing there.

"Ha, ha, you've had bad luck," said the operator—"you lose, you lose. Well, I'm sorry for you, old fellow, but we all take chances in this little game, you know." He was folding up his table when all of a sudden a cry arose to heaven from Schwalliger's lips, and he grappled with the very shrewd young man, while shriek on shriek of "Murder! Robber! Police!" came from his lips. The police at Bennings were not slow to answer a call like this, and they came running up, and Schwalliger, who, among other things, was something of an actor, told his story trembling, incoherently, while the operator looked on aghast. Schwalliger demanded protection. He had been robbed. He had bet his eighty-five dollars against the operator's forty, and when he had accidentally picked out the right shell the operator had grabbed his money and attempted to escape. He wanted his money. He had eighty-five dollars, he said. "He had fo' fiveth, fo' tenth, and five five-dollar gold-pieceth, an' he wanted them."

The policeman was thorough. He made his search at once. It was even as Schwalliger had said. The money was on the gambler even as the Negro had said. Well, there was nothing but justice to be done. The officers returned the eighty-five dollars to Schwalliger, and out of an unusual access of clemency bade the operator begone or they would run him in.

When he had gone, Schwalliger turned and winked slowly at the minions of the law, and went quietly into a corner with them, and there was the sound of the shuffling of silken paper. Later on he found the old man and returned him his ten, and went back to don his Jacob's coat.

Who shall say that Schwalliger was not a true philanthropist?

XIV

THE INTERFERENCE OF PATSY ANN

PATSY ANN MERIWEATHER would have told you that her father, or more properly her "pappy," was a "widover," and she would have added in her sad little voice, with her mournful eyes upon you, that her mother had "bin daid fu' nigh onto fou' yeahs." Then you could have wept for Patsy, for her years were only thirteen now, and since the passing away of her mother she had been the little mother for her four younger brothers and sisters, as well as her father's housekeeper.

But Patsy Ann never complained; she was quite willing to be all that she had been until such time as Isaac and Dora, Cassie and little John should be old enough to care for themselves, and also to lighten some of her domestic burdens. She had never reckoned upon any other manner of release. In fact her youthful mind was not able to contemplate the possibility of any other manner of change. But the good women of Patsy's neighbourhood were not the ones to let her remain in this deplorable state of ignorance. She was to be enlightened as to other changes that might take place in her condition, and of the unspeakable horrors that would transpire with them.

It was upon the occasion that little John had taken it into his infant head to have the German measles just at the time that Isaac was slowly recovering from the chicken-pox. Patsy Ann's powers had been taxed to the utmost, and Mrs. Caroline Gibson had been called in from next door to superintend the brewing of the saffron tea, and for the general care of the fretful sufferer.

To Patsy Ann, then, in ominous tone, spoke this oracle. "Patsy Ann, how yo' pappy doin' sence Matildy died?" "Matildy" was the deceased wife.

97

"Oh, he gittin' 'long all right. He was mighty broke up at de fus', but he 'low now dat de house go on de same's ef mammy was a-livin'."

"Oom huh," disdainfully; "Oom huh. Yo' mammy bin daid fou' yeahs, ain't she?"

"Yes'm; mighty nigh."

"Oom huh; fou' yeahs is a mighty long time fu' a colo'd man to wait; but we'n he do wait dat long, hit's all de wuss we'n hit do come."

"Pap bin wo'kin right stiddy at de brick-ya'd," said Patsy, in loyal defence against some vaguely implied accusation, "an' he done put some money in de bank."

"Bad sign, bad sign," and Mrs. Gibson gave her head a fearsome shake.

But just then the shrill voice of little John calling for attention drew her away and left Patsy Ann to herself and her meditations.

What could this mean?

When that lady had finished ministering to the sick child and returned, Patsy Ann asked her, "Mis' Gibson, what you mean by sayin' 'bad sign, bad sign?'"

Again the oracle shook her head sagely. Then she answered, "Chil', you do' know de dev'ment dey is in dis worl'."

"But," retorted the child, "my pappy ain' up to no dev'ment, 'case he got 'uligion an' bin baptised."

"Oom-m," groaned Sistah Gibson, "dat don' mek a bit o' diffunce. Who is any mo' ma'yin' men den de preachahs demse'ves? W'y Brothah 'Lias Scott done tempted matermony six times a'ready, an' 's lookin' roun' fu' de sebent, an' he's a good man, too."

"Ma'yin'," said Patsy breathlessly.

"Yes, honey, ma'yin', an' I's afeared yo' pappy's got notions in his haid, an' w'en a widower git gals in his haid dey ain' no use a-pesterin' wid 'em, 'case dey boun' to have dey way."

"Ma'yin'," said Patsy to herself reflectively. "Ma'yin'." She knew what it meant, but she had never dreamed of the possibility of such a thing in connection with her father. "Ma'yin'," and yet the idea of it did not seem so very unalluring.

She spoke her thoughts aloud.

"But ef pap 'u'd ma'y, Mis' Gibson, den I'd git a chanct to go to school. He allus sayin' he mighty sorry 'bout me not goin'."

"Dah now, dah now," cried the woman, casting a pitying glance at the child, "dat's de las' t'ing. He des a feelin' roun' now. You po', ign'ant, mothahless chil'. You ain' nevah had no step-mothah, an' you don' know what hit means."

"But she'd tek keer o' the chillen," persisted Patsy.

"Sich tekin' keer of 'em ez hit 'u'd be. She'd keer fu' 'em to dey graves. Nobody cain't tell me nuffin 'bout step-mothahs, case I knows 'em. Dey ain' no ooman goin' to tek keer o' nobody else's chile lak she'd tek keer o' huh own," and Patsy felt a choking come into her throat and a tight sensation about her heart while she listened as Mrs. Gibson regaled her with all the choice horrors that are laid at the door of step-mothers.

From that hour on, one settled conviction took shape and possessed Patsy Ann's mind; never, if she could help it, would she run the risk of having a step-mother. Come what may, let her be compelled to do what she might, let the hope of school fade from her sight forever and a day—but no step-mother should ever cast her baneful shadow over Patsy Ann's home.

Experience of life had made her wise for her years, and so for the time she said nothing to her father; but she began to watch him with wary eyes, his goings out and his comings in, and to attach new importance to trifles that had passed unnoticed before by her childish mind.

For instance, if he greased or blacked his boots before going out of an evening her suspicions were immediately aroused and she saw dim visions of her father returning, on his arm the terrible ogress whom she had come to know by the name of step-mother.

Mrs. Gibson's poison had worked well and rapidly. She had thoroughly inoculated the child's mind with the step-mother virus, but she had not at the same time made the parent widow-proof, a hard thing to do at best. So it came to pass that with a mysterious horror growing within her, Patsy Ann saw her father black his boots more and more often and fare forth o' nights and Sunday afternoons.

Finally her little heart could contain its sorrow no longer, and one night when he was later than usual she could not sleep. So she slipped out of bed, turned up the light, and waited for him, determined to have it out, then and there.

He came at last and was all surprise to meet the solemn, round eyes of his little daughter staring at him from across the table.

"W'y, lady gal," he exclaimed, "what you doin' up at 'his time?"

"I sat up fu' you. I got somep'n' to ax you, pappy." Her voice quivered and he snuggled her up in his arms.

"What's troublin' my little lady gal now? Is de chillen bin bad?"

She laid her head close against his big breast, and the tears would come as she answered, "No, suh; de chillen bin ez good az good could be, but oh, pappy, pappy, is you got gal in yo' haid an' a-goin' to bring me a step-mothah?"

He held her away from him almost harshly and gazed at her as he queried, "W'y, you po' baby, you! Who's bin puttin' dis hyeah foolishness in yo' haid?" Then his laugh rang out as he patted her head and drew her close to him again. "Ef yo' pappy do bring a step-mothah into dis house, Gawd knows he'll bring de right kin'."

"Dey ain't no right kin'," answered Patsy.

"You don' know, baby; you don' know. Go to baid an' don' worry."

He sat up a long time watching the candle sputter, then he pulled off his boots and tiptoed to Patsy's bedside. He leaned over her. "Po' little baby," he said; "what do she know about a step-mothah?" And Patsy saw him and heard him, for she was awake then, and far into the night.

In the eyes of the child her father stood convicted. He had "gal in his haid," and was going to bring her a step-mother; but it would never be; her resolution was taken.

She arose early the next morning and after getting her father off to work as usual, she took the children into hand. First she scrubbed them assiduously, burnishing their brown faces until they shone again. Then she tussled with their refractory locks, and after that she dressed them out in all the bravery of their best clothes.

Meanwhile her tears were falling like rain, though her lips were shut tight. The children off her mind, she turned her attention to her own toilet, which she made with scrupulous care. Then taking a small tin-type of her mother from the bureau drawer, she put it in her bosom, and leading her little brood she went out of the house, locking the door behind her and placing the key, as was her wont, under the door-step.

Outside she stood for a moment or two, undecided, and then with one long, backward glance at her home she turned and went up the street. At the first corner she paused again, spat in her hand and struck the watery globule with her finger. In the direction the most of the spittle flew, she turned. Patsy Ann was fleeing from home and a step-mother, and Fate had decided her direction for her, even as Mrs. Gibson's counsels had directed her course.

The child had no idea where she was going. She knew no one to whom she might turn in her distress. Not even with Mrs. Gibson would she be safe from the horror which impended. She had but one impulse in her mind and that was to get beyond the reach of the terrible woman, or was it a monster? who was surely coming after her. On and on she walked through the town with her little band trudging bravely along beside her. People turned to look at the funny group and smiled good-naturedly as they passed, and one man, a little more amused than the rest, shouted after them, "Where you goin', sis, with that orphan's home?"

But Patsy Ann's dignity was impregnable. She walked on with her head in the air, the desire for safety tugging at her heart.

The hours passed and the gentle coolness of morning turned into the fierce heat of noon, and still with frequent rests they trudged on, Patsy ever and anon using her divining hand, unconscious that she was doubling and redoubling on her tracks. When the whistles blew for twelve she got her little brood into the shade of a poplar tree and set them down to the lunch which, thoughtful little mother that she was, she had brought with her. After that they all stretched themselves out on the grass that bordered the sidewalk, for all the children were tired out, and baby John was both sleepy and cross. Even Patsy Ann drowsed and finally dropped into the deep slumber of childhood. They looked too peaceful and serene for passers-by to bother them, and so they slept and slept.

It was past three o'clock when the little guardian awakened with a start, and shook her charges into activity. John wept a little at first, but after a while took up his journey bravely with the rest.

She had just turned into a side street, discouraged and bewildered, when the round face of a coloured woman standing in the doorway of a whitewashed cottage caught her eye and attention. Once more she paused and consulted her watery oracle, then turned to encounter the gaze of the round-faced woman. The oracle had spoken and she turned into the yard.

"Whaih you goin', honey? You sut'ny look lak you plumb tukahed out. Come in an' tell me all 'bout yo'se'f, you po' little t'ing. Dese yo' little brothas an' sistahs?"

"Yes'm," said Patsy Ann.

"W'y, chil', whaih you goin'?"

"I don' know," was the truthful answer.

"You don' know? Whaih you live?"

"Oh, I live down on Douglas Street," said Patsy Ann, "an' I's runnin' away f'om home an' my step-mothah."

The woman looked keenly at her.

"What yo' name?" she said.

"My name's Patsy Ann Meriweather."

"An' is yo' got a step-mothah?"

"No," said Patsy Ann, "I ain' got none now, but I's sut'ny 'spectin' one."

"What you know 'bout step-mothahs, honey?"

"Mis' Gibson tol' me. Dey sho'ly is awful, missus, awful."

"Mis' Gibson ain' tol' you right, honey. You come in hyeah and set down. You ain' nothin' mo' dan a baby yo'se'f, an' you ain' got no right to be trapsein' roun' dis away."

Have you ever eaten muffins? Have you eaten bacon with onions? Have you drunk tea? Have you seen your little brother John taken up on a full bosom and rocked to sleep in the most motherly way, with the sweetness and tenderness that only a mother can give? Well, that was Patsy Ann's case to-night.

And then she laid them along like ten-pins crosswise of her bed and sat for a long time thinking.

To Maria Adams about six o'clock that night came a troubled and disheartened man. It was no less a person than Patsy Ann's father.

"Maria! Maria! What shall I do? Somebody don' stole all my chillen."

Maria, strange to say, was a woman of few words.

"Don' you bothah 'bout de chillen," she said, and she took him by the hand and led him to where the five lay sleeping calmly across the bed.

"Dey was runnin' f'om home an' dey step-mothah," said she.

"Dey run hyeah f'om a step-mothah an' foun' a mothah." It was a tribute and a proposal all in one.

When Patsy Ann awakened, the matter was explained to her, and with penitent tears she confessed her sins.

"But," she said to Maria Adams, "ef you's de kin' of fo'ks dat dey mek step-mothahs out o' I ain' gwine to bothah my haid no mo'."

XV

THE HOME-COMING
OF 'RASTUS SMITH

THERE WAS A GREAT COMMOTION in that part of town which was known as "Little Africa," and the cause of it was not far to seek. Contrary to the usual thing, this cause was not an excursion down the river, nor a revival, baptising, nor an Emancipation Day celebration. None of these was it that had aroused the denizens of "Little Africa," and kept them talking across the street from window to window, from door to door, through alley gates, over backyard fences, where they stood loud-mouthed and arms akimboed among laden clothes lines. No, the cause of it all was that Erastus Smith, Aunt Mandy Smith's boy, who had gone away from home several years before, and who, rumour said, had become a great man, was coming back, and "Little Africa," from Douglass Street to Cat Alley, was prepared to be dazzled. So few of those who had been born within the mile radius which was "Little Africa" went out into the great world and came into contact with the larger humanity that when one did he became a man set apart. And when, besides, he went into a great city and worked for a lawyer whose name was known the country over, the place of his birth had all the more reason to feel proud of her son.

So there was much talk across the dirty little streets, and Aunt Mandy's small house found itself all of a sudden a very popular resort. The old women held Erastus up as an example to their sons. The old men told what they might have done had they had his chance. The young men cursed him, and the young girls giggled and waited.

It was about an hour before the time of the arrival of Erastus, and the neighbours had thinned out one by one with a delicacy rather surprising in them, in order that the old lady might be alone with her boy for the first few minutes. Only one remained to help put the finishing touches to the two little rooms which Mrs. Smith called home, and to the preparations for the great dinner. The old woman wiped her eyes as she said to her companion, "Hit do seem a speshul blessin', Lizy, dat I been spaihed to see dat chile once mo' in de flesh. He sholy was mighty nigh to my hea't, an' w'en he went erway, I thought it 'ud kill me. But I kin see now dat hit uz all fu' de bes'. Think o' 'Rastus comin' home, er big man! Who'd evah 'specked dat?"

"Law, Mis' Smif, you sholy is got reason to be mighty thankful. Des' look how many young men dere is in dis town what ain't nevah been no 'count to dey pa'ents, ner anybody else."

"Well, it's onexpected, Lizy, an' hit's 'spected. 'Rastus allus wuz a wonnerful chil', an' de way he tuk to work an' study kin' o' promised something f'om de commencement, an' I 'lowed mebbe he tu'n out a preachah."

"Tush! yo' kin thank yo' stahs he didn't tu'n out no preachah. Preachahs ain't no bettah den anybody else dese days. Dey des go roun' tellin' dey lies an' eatin' de whiders an' orphins out o' house an' home."

"Well, mebbe hit's bes' he didn't tu'n out dat way. But f'om de way he used to stan' on de chaih an' 'zort w'en he was a little boy, I thought hit was des what he 'ud tu'n out. O' co'se, being' in a law office is des as pervidin', but somehow hit do seem mo' worl'y."

"Didn't I tell you de preachahs is ez worldly ez anybody else?"

"Yes, yes, dat's right, but den 'Rastus, he had de eddication, fo' he had gone thoo de Third Readah."

Just then the gate creaked, and a little brown-faced girl, with large, mild eyes, pushed open the door and came shyly in.

"Hyeah's some flowahs, Mis' Smif," she said. "I thought mebbe you might like to decorate 'Rastus's room," and she wiped the confusion from her face with her apron.

"La, chil', thankee. Dese is mighty pu'tty posies." These were the laurels which Sally Martin had brought to lay at the feet of her home-coming hero. No one in Cat Alley but that queer, quiet little girl would have thought of decorating anybody's room with flowers, but she had peculiar notions.

In the old days, when they were children, and before Erastus had gone away to become great, they had gone up and down together along the byways of their locality, and had loved as children love. Later, when Erastus began keeping company, it was upon Sally that he bestowed his affections. No one, not even her mother, knew how she had waited for him all these years that he had been gone, few in reality, but so long and so many to her.

And now he was coming home. She scorched something in the ironing that day because tears of joy were blinding her eyes. Her thoughts were busy with the meeting that was to be. She had a brand new dress for the occasion—a lawn, with dark blue dots, and a blue sash—and there was a new hat, wonderful with the flowers of summer, and for both of them she had spent her hard-earned savings, because she wished to be radiant in the eyes of the man who loved her.

Of course, Erastus had not written her; but he must have been busy, and writing was hard work. She knew that herself, and realised it all the more as she penned the loving little scrawls which at first she used to send him. Now they would not have to do any writing any more; they could say what they wanted to each other. He was coming home at last, and she had waited long.

They paint angels with shining faces and halos, but for real radiance one should have looked into the dark eyes of Sally as she sped home after her contribution to her lover's reception.

When the last one of the neighbours had gone Aunt Mandy sat down to rest herself and to await the great event. She had not sat there long before the gate creaked. She arose and hastened to the window. A young man was coming down the path. Was that 'Rastus? Could that be her 'Rastus, that gorgeous creature with the shiny shoes and the nobby suit and the carelessly-swung cane? But he was knocking at her door, and she opened it and took him into her arms.

"Why, howdy, honey, howdy; hit do beat all to see you agin, a great big, grown-up man. You're lookin' des' lak one o' de big folks up in town."

Erastus submitted to her endearments with a somewhat condescending grace, as who should say, "Well, poor old fool, let her go on this time; she doesn't know any better." He smiled superiorly when the old woman wept glad tears, as mothers have a way of doing over returned sons, however great fools these sons may be. She set him down to the dinner which she had prepared for him, and with loving patience drew from his pompous and reluctant lips some of the story of his doings and some little word about the places he had seen.

"Oh, yes," he said, crossing his legs, "as soon as Mr. Carrington saw that I was pretty bright, he took me right up and gave me a good job, and I have been working for him right straight along for seven years now. Of course, it don't do to let white folks know all you're thinking; but I have kept my ears and my eyes right open, and I guess I know just about as much about law as he does himself. When I save up a little more I'm going to put on the finishing touches and hang out my shingle."

"Don't you nevah think no mo' 'bout bein' a preachah, 'Rastus?" his mother asked.

"Haw, haw! Preachah? Well, I guess not; no preaching in mine; there's nothing in it. In law you always have a chance to get into politics and be the president of your ward club or something like that, and from that on it's an easy matter to go on up. You can trust me to know the wires." And so the tenor of his boastful talk ran on, his mother a little bit awed and not altogether satisfied with the new 'Rastus that had returned to her.

He did not stay in long that evening, although his mother told him some of the neighbours were going to drop in. He said he wanted to go about and see something of the town. He paused just long enough to glance at the flowers in his room, and to his mother's remark, "Sally Ma'tin brung dem in," he returned answer, "Who on earth is Sally Martin?"

"Why, 'Rastus," exclaimed his mother, "does yo' 'tend lak yo' don't 'member little Sally Ma'tin yo' used to go wid almos' f'om de time you was babies? W'y, I'm s'prised at you."

"She has slipped my mind," said the young man.

For a long while the neighbours who had come and Aunt Mandy sat up to wait for Erastus, but he did not come in until the last one was gone. In fact, he did not get in until nearly four o'clock in the morning, looking a little weak, but at least in the best of spirits, and he vouchsafed to his waiting mother the remark that "the little old town wasn't so bad, after all."

Aunt Mandy preferred the request that she had had in mind for some time, that he would go to church the next day, and he consented, because his trunk had come.

It was a glorious Sunday morning, and the old lady was very

proud in her stiff gingham dress as she saw her son come into the room arrayed in his long coat, shiny hat, and shinier shoes. Well, if it was true that he was changed, he was still her 'Rastus, and a great comfort to her. There was no vanity about the old woman, but she paused before the glass a longer time than usual, settling her bonnet strings, for she must look right, she told herself, to walk to church with that elegant son of hers. When he was all ready, with cane in hand, and she was pausing with the key in the door, he said, "Just walk on, mother, I'll catch you in a minute or two." She went on and left him.

He did not catch her that morning on her way to church, and it was a sore disappointment, but it was somewhat compensated for when she saw him stalking into the chapel in all his glory, and every head in the house turned to behold him.

There was one other woman in "Little Africa" that morning who stopped for a longer time than usual before her looking-glass and who had never found her bonnet strings quite so refractory before. In spite of the vexation of flowers that wouldn't settle and ribbons that wouldn't tie, a very glad face looked back at Sally Martin from her little mirror. She was going to see 'Rastus, 'Rastus of the old days in which they used to walk hand in hand. He had told her when he went away that some day he would come back and marry her. Her heart fluttered hotly under her dotted lawn, and it took another application of the chamois to take the perspiration from her face. People had laughed at her, but that morning she would be vindicated. He would walk home with her before the whole church. Already she saw him bowing before her, hat in hand, and heard the set phrase, "May I have the pleasure of your company home?" and she saw herself sailing away upon his arm.

She was very happy as she sat in church that morning, as happy as Mrs. Smith herself, and as proud when she saw the object of her affections swinging up the aisle to the collection table, and from the ring she knew that it could not be less than a half dollar that he put in.

There was a special note of praise in her voice as she joined in singing the doxology that morning, and her heart kept quivering and fluttering like a frightened bird as the people gathered in groups, chattering and shaking hands, and he drew nearer to her. Now they were almost together; in a moment their eyes would meet. Her breath came quickly; he had looked at her, surely he must have seen her. His mother was just behind him, and he did not speak. Maybe she had changed, maybe he had forgotten her. An unaccustomed boldness took possession of her, and she determined that she would not be overlooked. She pressed forward. She saw his mother take his arm and heard her whisper, "Dere's Sally Ma'tin" this time, and she knew that he looked at her. He bowed as if to a stranger, and was past her the next minute. When she saw him again he was swinging out of the door between two admiring lines of church-goers who separated on the pavement. There was a brazen yellow girl on his arm.

She felt weak and sick as she hid behind the crowd as well as she could, and for that morning she thanked God that she was small.

Aunt Mandy trudged home alone, and when the street was cleared and the sexton was about to lock up, the girl slipped out of the church and down to her own little house. In the friendly shelter of her room she took off her gay attire and laid it away, and then sat down at the window and looked dully out. For her, the light of day had gone out.

XVI

THE BOY AND THE BAYONET

IT WAS JUNE, and nearing the closing time of school. The air was full of the sound of bustle and preparation for the final exercises, field day, and drills. Drills especially, for nothing so gladdens the heart of the Washington mother, be she black or white, as seeing her boy in the blue cadet's uniform, marching proudly to the huzzas of an admiring crowd. Then she forgets the many nights when he has come in tired out and dusty from his practice drill, and feels only the pride and elation of the result.

Although Tom did all he could outside of study hours, there were many days of hard work for Hannah Davis, when her son went into the High School. But she took it upon herself gladly, since it gave Bud the chance to learn, that she wanted him to have. When, however, he entered the Cadet Corps it seemed to her as if the first steps toward the fulfilment of all her hopes had been made. It was a hard pull to her, getting the uniform, but Bud himself helped manfully, and when his mother saw him rigged out in all his regimentals, she felt that she had not toiled in vain. And in fact it was worth all the trouble and expense just to see the joy and pride of "little sister," who adored Bud.

As the time for the competitive drill drew near there was an air of suppressed excitement about the little house on "D" Street, where the three lived. All day long "little sister," who was never very well and did not go to school, sat and looked out of the window on the uninteresting prospect of a dusty thoroughfare lined on either side with dull red brick houses, all of the same ugly pattern, interspersed with older, uglier, and viler frame shanties. In the evening Hannah hurried home to get supper against the time when Bud should return, hungry and tired from his drilling, and the chore work which followed hard upon its heels.

Things were all cheerful, however, for as they applied themselves to the supper, the boy, with glowing face, would tell just how his company "A" was getting on, and what they were going to do to companies "B" and "C." It was not boasting so much as the expression of a confidence, founded upon the hard work he was doing, and Hannah and the "little sister" shared that with him.

The child often, listening to her brother, would clap her hands or cry, "Oh, Bud, you're just splendid an' I know you'll beat 'em."

"If hard work'll beat 'em, we've got 'em beat," Bud would reply, and Hannah, to add an admonitory check to her own confidence, would break in with, "Now, don't you be too sho', son; dey ain't been no man so good dat dey wasn't somebody bettah." But all the while her face and manner were disputing what her words expressed.

The great day came, and it was a wonderful crowd of people that packed the great baseball grounds to overflowing. It seemed that all of Washington's coloured population was out, when there were really only about one-tenth of them there. It was an enthusiastic, banner-waving, shouting, hallooing crowd. Its component parts were strictly and frankly partisan, and so separated themselves into sections differentiated by the colours of the flags they carried and the ribbons they wore. Side yelled defiance at side, and party bantered party. Here the blue and white of Company "A" flaunted audaciously on the breeze beside the very seats over which the crimson and gray of "B" were flying, and these in their turn nodded defiance over the imaginary barrier between themselves and "C's" black and yellow.

The band was thundering out "Sousa's High School Cadet's March," the school officials, the judges, and reporters, and some with less purpose were bustling about, discussing and conferring. Altogether doing nothing much with beautiful unanimity. All was noise, hurry, gaiety, and turbulence. In the midst of it all, with blue and white rosettes pinned on their breasts, sat two spectators, tense and silent, while the breakers of movement and sound struck and broke around them. It meant too much to Hannah and "little sister" for them to laugh and shout. Bud was with Company "A," and so the whole programme was more like a religious ceremonial to them. The blare of the brass to them might have been the trumpet call to battle in old Judea, and the far-thrown tones of the megaphone the voice of a prophet proclaiming from the hill-top.

Hannah's face glowed with expectation, and "little sister" sat very still and held her mother's hand save when amid a burst of cheers Company "A" swept into the parade ground at a quick step, then she sprang up, crying shrilly, "There's Bud, there's Bud, I see him," and then settled back into her seat overcome with embarrassment. The mother's eyes danced as soon as the sister's had singled out their dear one from the midst of the blue-coated boys, and it was an effort for her to keep from following her little daughter's example even to echoing her words.

Company "A" came swinging down the field toward the judges in a manner that called for more enthusiastic huzzas that carried even the Freshman of other commands "off their feet." They were, indeed, a set of fine-looking young fellows, brisk, straight, and soldierly in bearing. Their captain was proud of them, and his very step showed it. He was like a skilled operator pressing the key of some great mechanism, and at his command they moved like clockwork. Seen from the side it was as if they were all bound together by inflexible iron bars, and as the end man moved all must move with him. The crowd was full of exclamations of praise and admiration, but a tense quiet enveloped them as Company "A" came from columns of four into line for volley firing. This was a real test; it meant not only grace and precision of movement, singleness of attention and steadiness, but quickness tempered by self-control. At the command the volley rang forth like a single shot. This was again the signal for wild cheering and the blue and white streamers kissed the sunlight with swift impulsive kisses. Hannah and Little Sister drew closer together and pressed hands.

The "A" adherents, however, were considerably cooled when the next volley came out, badly scattering, with one shot entirely apart and before the rest. Bud's mother did not entirely understand the sudden quieting of the adherents; they felt vaguely that all was not as it should be, and the chill of fear laid hold upon their hearts. What if Bud's company, (it was always Bud's company to them), what if his company should lose. But, of course, that couldn't be. Bud himself had said that they would win. Suppose, though, they didn't; and with these thoughts they were miserable until the cheering again told them that the company had redeemed itself.

Someone behind Hannah said, "They are doing splendidly, they'll win, they'll win yet in spite of the second volley."

Company "A", in columns of fours, had executed the right oblique in double time, and halted amid cheers; then formed left halt into line without halting. The next movement was one looked forward to with much anxiety on account of its difficulty. The order was marching by fours to fix or unfix bayonets. They were going at a quick step, but the boys' hands were steady—hope was bright in their hearts. They were doing it rapidly and freely, when suddenly from the ranks there was the bright gleam of steel lower down than it should have been. A gasp broke from the breasts of Company "A's" friends. The blue and white drooped disconsolately, while a few heartless ones who wore other colours attempted to hiss. Someone had dropped his bayonet. But with muscles unquivering, without a turned head, the company moved on as if nothing had happened, while one of the judges, an army officer, stepped into the wake of the boys and picked up the fallen steel.

No two eyes had seen half so quickly as Hannah and Little Sister's who the blunderer was. In the whole drill there had been but one figure for them, and that was Bud, Bud, and it was he who had dropped his bayonet. Anxious, nervous with the desire to please them, perhaps with a shade too much of thought of them looking on with their hearts in their eyes, he had fumbled, and lost all that he was striving for. His head went round and round and all seemed black before him.

He executed the movements in a dazed way. The applause, generous and sympathetic, as his company left the parade ground, came to him from afar off, and like a wounded animal he crept away from his comrades, not because their reproaches stung him, for he did not hear them, but because he wanted to think what his mother and "Little Sister" would say, but his misery was as nothing to that of the two who sat up there amid the ranks of the blue and white holding each other's hands with a despairing grip. To Bud all of the rest of the contest was a horrid nightmare; he hardly knew when the three companies were marched back to receive the judges' decision. The applause that greeted Company "B" when the blue ribbons were pinned on the members' coats meant nothing to his ears. He had disgraced himself and his company. What would his mother and his "Little Sister" say?

To Hannah and "Little Sister," as to Bud, all of the remainder of the drill was a misery. The one interest they had had in it failed, and not even the dropping of his gun by one of Company "E" when on the march, halting in line, could raise their spirits. The little girl tried to be brave, but when it was all over she was glad to hurry out before the crowd got started and to hasten away home. Once there and her tears flowed freely; she hid her face in her mother's dress, and sobbed as if her heart would break.

"Don't cry, Baby! don't cry, Lammie, dis ain't da las' time da wah goin' to be a drill. Bud 'll have a chance anotha time and den he'll show 'em somethin'; bless you, I spec' he'll be a captain." But this consolation of philosophy was nothing to "Little Sister." It was so terrible to her, this failure of Bud's. She couldn't blame him, she couldn't blame anyone else, and she had not yet learned to lay all such unfathomed catastrophes at the door of fate. What to her was the thought of another day; what did it matter to her whether he was a captain or a private? She didn't even know the meaning of the words, but "Little Sister," from the time she knew Bud was a private, that that was much better than being captain or any of those other things with a long name, so that settled it.

Her mother finally set about getting the supper, while "Little Sister" drooped disconsolately in her own little splint-bottomed chair. She sat there weeping silently until she heard the sound of Bud's step, then she sprang up and ran away to hide. She didn't dare to face him with tears in her eyes. Bud came in without a word and sat down in the dark front room.

"Dat you, Bud?" asked his mother.

"Yassum."

"Bettah come now, supper's puty 'nigh ready."

"I don' want no supper."

"You bettah come on, Bud, I reckon you mighty tired."

He did not reply, but just then a pair of thin arms were put around his neck and a soft cheek was placed close to his own.

"Come on, Buddie," whispered "Little Sister," "Mammy an' me know you didn't mean to do it, an' we don' keer."

Bud threw his arms around his little sister and held her tightly.

"It's only you an' ma I care about," he said, "though I am sorry I spoiled the company's drill; they say "B" would have won anyway on account of our bad firing, but I did want you and ma to be proud."

"We is proud," she whispered, "we's mos' prouder dan if you'd won," and pretty soon she led him by the hand out to supper.

Hannah did all she could to cheer the boy and to encourage him to hope for next year, but he had little to say in reply, and went to bed early.

In the morning, though it neared school time, Bud lingered around and seemed in no disposition to get ready to go.

"Bettah git ready fer school," said Hannah cheerily to him.

"I don't believe I want to go any more," Bud replied.

"Not go any more? Why ain't you shamed to talk that way! O' cose you a goin' to school."

"I'm ashamed to show my face to the boys."

"What you say about de boys? De boys ain't a-goin' to give you no edgication when you need it."

"Oh, I don't want to go, ma; you don't know how I feel."

"I'm kinder sorry I let you go into dat company," said Hannah musingly; "'cause it was de teachin' I wanted you to git, not de prancin' and steppin'; but I did t'ink it would make mo' of a man of you, an' it ain't. Yo' pappy was a po' man, ha'd wo'kin', an' he wasn't high-toned neither, but from the time I first see him to the day of his death I nevah seen him back down because he was afeared of anything," and Hannah turned to her work.

"Little Sister" went up to Bud and slipped her hand in his. "You ain't a-goin' to back down, is you, Buddie?" she said.

"No," said Bud stoutly, as he braced his shoulders, "I'm a-goin'."

But no persuasion could make him wear his uniform.

The boys were a little cold to him, and some were brutal. But most of them recognised the fact that what had happened to Tom Harris might have happened to any one of them. Besides, since the percentage had been shown, it was found that "B" had outpointed them in many ways, and so their loss was not due to the one grave error. Bud's heart sank when he dropped into his seat in the Assembly Hall to find seated on the platform one of the blue-coated officers who had acted as judge the day before. After the opening exercises were over he was called upon to address the school. He spoke readily and pleasantly, laying especial stress upon the value of discipline; toward the end of his address he said: "I suppose Company 'A' is heaping accusations upon the head of the young man who dropped his bayonet yesterday." Tom could have died. "It was most regrettable," the officer continued, "but to me the most significant thing at the drill was the conduct of that cadet afterward. I saw the whole proceeding; I saw that he did not pause for an instant, that he did not even turn his head, and it appeared to me as one of the finest bits of self-control I had ever seen in any youth; had he forgotten himself for a moment and stopped, however quickly, to secure the weapon, the next line would have been interfered with and your whole movement thrown into confusion." There were a half hundred eyes glancing furtively at Bud, and the light began to dawn in his face. "This boy has shown what discipline means, and I for one want to shake hands with him, if he is here."

When he had concluded the Principal called Bud forward, and the boys, even his detractors, cheered as the officer took his hand.

"Why are you not in uniform, sir?" he asked.

"I was ashamed to wear it after yesterday," was the reply.

"Don't be ashamed to wear your uniform," the officer said to him, and Bud could have fallen on his knees and thanked him.

There were no more jeers from his comrades now, and when he related it all at home that evening there were two more happy hearts in that South Washington cottage.

"I told you we was more prouder dan if you'd won," said "Little Sister."

"An' what did I tell you 'bout backin' out?" asked his mother.

Bud was too happy and too busy to answer; he was brushing his uniform.

THE END